WELCOME BACK, CARTER

2004 DEMOCRATIC PRESIDENTIAL POLL WINNER

BY

EARL CLARK COLEMAN

ISBN: 1-4140-3199-8 (e-book)
ISBN: 1-4140-3200-5 (Paperback)
ISBN: 1-4140-3201-3 (Dust Jacket)

This book is printed on acid free paper.

1stBooks - rev. 12/10/03

100% of the author's proceeds will be donated to the Carter Center, a 501c(3) non-profit organization. President Carter and the Carter Center did not authorize, nor were informed, about the publishing of *Welcome Back, Carter*. The Atlanta Journal-Constitution cover photo does not represent an endorsement of the views set forth in this book.

To individual Democrats and independents, that they may be made aware of their surprising collective choice for the 2004 Democratic presidential nomination, Jimmy Carter—the peanut farmer—nuclear engineer—Sunday school teacher—governor—peace wager—disease fighter—carpenter—human rights champion—election monitor—author—Nobel Laureate—President of the United States whose stature on the world stage is unmatched by any American.

CONTENTS

PROLOGUE

Even though *Welcome Back, Carter* is a relatively short book, it is long on facts, because of the extended record of achievement of Jimmy Carter, the 39th president of the United States and the 2002 Nobel Peace Prize recipient. Here is the first fact: a CBS News poll in September of 2003 indicated that two-thirds of the electorate were unable to name even one of the candidates vying for the 2004 Democratic presidential nomination—which I roughly knew to be the case long before by virtue of unscientific but in-person nationwide field surveys that I conducted over a several month period. Political commentators have lamented a lack of stature among any of the Democratic candidates, which reportedly left Democratic Party officials pining for a last-minute entry into the race by New York Senator Hillary Clinton, despite her statements to the contrary. Yet based on my poll findings that saw Carter as the favorite—which quite frankly floored me because of his advanced years—and after absorbing a long list of his accomplishments in both his post-presidency and his term in office, I came to the inescapable conclusion that the seemingly ageless Carter would indeed be the Democrats' strongest possible opponent for George W. Bush in 2004. By his rank as a former president, I contend that Carter's stature easily surpasses that of retired General Wesley Clark, who entered the race long after my polls were conducted, and immediately bested the Democratic field in a national poll shortly after his declaration.

The passage of a generation has revealed Carter to be a latter-day Harry Truman, with both pursuing policies in office that proved to be ahead of their time in many respects. On top of that, Carter's post-presidential works in promoting peace, spreading democracy, and eradicating disease in Africa are without precedent. No one can deny Carter's setbacks as president, but it's interesting how the raging inflation that marred Truman's second term and dropped his approval ratings into the ditch while still in office didn't permanently define his presidency in a negative light, nor did the stalemate in Korea. Supporters of George W. Bush note that the loss of nearly three million jobs since he became president can be traced to the sluggish economy that he inherited from Bill Clinton. Carter also inherited an OPEC-driven slumping economy from the Nixon and Ford Administrations, and, like Bush, saw it bottom out under his watch. And while Carter was consumed during his final year in office by the Iranian hostage crisis, in the end he did get them all out alive.

In the ensuing chapters, I will attempt to reinforce the essential points others have made about Carter: that he's the furthest thing from an economic liberal (note his constant policy battles with Ted Kennedy); that he is a swift decision-maker, irregardless of the polls, in the vein of Truman; that the military was strengthened under his watch, not weakened, as Republicans have endlessly repeated in face of the facts; that he was the first president to challenge the legitimacy of the Soviet Union; and that he is a man of unquestionable courage, as evidenced by his 1994 mission in Haiti that will be described in the introduction. The ultimate issue that *Welcome Back, Carter* seeks to raise is self-evident: *would Jimmy Carter make himself available for his party's 2004 nomination if professional pollsters verified that he would indeed be the leading choice of Democrats and independents if he became an announced candidate?*

It may be possible to answer that question by picturing this scenario. It's the early spring of 2004, and no clear-cut leader has emerged among the top Democratic contenders through the early primaries. Legitimate polls that include Carter as a hypothetical candidate show a level of support for the former president that strongly suggests that he'd be the prohibitive favorite to capture the nomination if he sought it. Carter finally agrees to appear on *Larry King Live*; based on the findings of the polls, King alludes to the inevitability of Carter's nomination if Carter desired it.

"You know," says King, "These numbers show that most Democrats want you to be the one to take on George W. Bush in November. We're talking about the possibility of an historic campaign pitting a former president against the incumbent. So, the obvious question is, do you want to put an end to the speculation tonight, and announce you will not run, or are you willing to answer the call of millions of Democrats throughout the nation and once again seek your party's nomination—and if successful, attempt to complete the greatest comeback in American political history by being re-elected president of the United States nearly a quarter century after your first term in office?"

What would Carter say in reply? That's anyone's guess, but I think an indication of his response can be found in the cover photo of *Welcome Back, Carter*.

That looks to me like a man who could say yes.

INTRODUCTION

In September of 1994, former President Jimmy Carter led a three-man delegation to Haiti for the purpose of brokering a peaceful departure of the Caribbean nation's military regime. Failure to reach an agreement would result in an immediate U.S. military intervention to reinstate departed president Jean-Bertrand Aristide, with the inevitable heavy price of casualties among U.S servicemen and Haitian civilians.

During the 11th-hour negotiations, former President Carter—who was joined by former Joint Chiefs of Staff Chairman Colin Powell and Georgia Senator Sam Nunn—was nearing a final settlement with Haiti's dictator Raoul Cedras that would ensure the ruler's safe exile. At that moment, a Haitian commander charged into the negotiating room, and waved a submarine gun at Carter, Powell, and Nunn, while informing Cedras that their military intelligence revealed that a U.S. invasion had already begun.

As Douglas Brinkley relates in his book, *The Unfinished Presidency*, Carter stared down the gunman and demanded that Cedras accept the proposed offer immediately or else face certain death and widespread destruction of his country. Powell, wrote Brinkley, was amazed at the courageous and forceful display by Jimmy Carter. "There was such power in his presentation," Powell stated. "He was tougher than I had thought." History shows that Carter and his team left Haiti with an agreement in hand. As Brinkley noted, the deal permitted the U.S. military "…to enter Haiti as friendly occupiers rather than hostile invaders."

Carter's achievement in Haiti should have put an end once and for all to the perception of many that he lacked the toughness required in a U.S. president. Carter enforced his will in Haiti even while looking down the barrel of a gun; if that doesn't convince Democratic and independent voters that the 2002 Nobel Peace Prize winner is also a man of uncommon strength, then nothing will.

What is the connection between *Welcome Back, Carter: 2004 Democratic Presidential Poll Winner* and Carter's diplomatic triumph in Haiti? If a man with the stature of Colin Powell was able to admit that he underestimated the strength of Jimmy Carter, then those who agreed with Powell's previous assessment of Carter all have reason to reconsider their opinion. Apparently, many have reconsidered; while I knew Carter was widely respected, the results that transpired from a little hobby of mine showed a greater level of support for the former president than I think anyone has previously determined.

When I began canvassing voters one-on-one throughout the country about their preference for the 2004 Democratic nomination, it definitely wasn't with the intent of writing a book about my experience. I've been doing informal surveys of the public in every presidential election cycle since 1988, first because of an avid interest in politics, and secondly, as a means to combat boredom while away from home on business trips. I've always been intrigued as to whether the unscientific polls I've conducted would basically approximate the general election vote totals, and I've taken pride that my results have fairly closely mirrored three of the four elections since 1988, coming within 3 points each time except in 1992, when my statistics just prior to the election found that Ross Perot's support had dropped to 9%, with most of his former supporters indicating their preference for Bill Clinton. Network exit polls in '92 indicated that a sizeable percentage of former Perot backers did switch to Clinton, but not in the vast numbers that I'd tallied. The actual results were: Clinton 43%, Bush 38%, and Perot 19%; my results were Clinton 49%, Bush 41%, and Perot 9%. So while I correctly forecast a Clinton win, the dimensions of the victory were somewhat overstated. But my surveys were close to the mark in the other three elections. In 1988, I had George H.W. Bush at 57% and Michael Dukakis 42% (actual totals: Bush 55%, Dukakis 44%); in 1996, I had Clinton at 52%, Dole 41%, and Perot 6% (actual totals: Clinton 49%, Dole 41%, and Perot 8%); and in 2000, I had George W. Bush at 50%, Al Gore at 47%, and Ralph Nader at 2% (actual totals: Bush 48%, Gore 48%, and Nader 3%).

This time around, though, instead of waiting to poll voters on the 2004 match-up between President Bush and his Democratic opponent, I thought I'd try something different and conduct a survey on voter preferences for the 2004 Democratic nominee, among the nine declared candidates as of February, 2003. You'll soon learn how my informal polling about the announced Democratic field evolved into a stunning discovery: that a plurality of Democrats and swing voters would give their vote to former President Carter, if he made an historic bid for a second term. The irony is that virtually every voter who cited Carter as their first choice had two basic assumptions: one, that he or she believed no one else besides themselves would cite Carter as their preference, and two, that it wouldn't matter because Carter would never consider running because of his advanced years.

With Carter finishing ahead of the Democratic field, I thought it would be logical to review his record and see exactly how much he's accomplished, both as president and in his post-presidency. The Carter Center Web Site was utilized as the source for his post-presidential record, which explains why I've earmarked 100% of the author's proceeds to the Carter Center. There seems to be a general consensus, even among Republicans, that Carter's post-presidency is the most impressive of any former president. With that in mind, I thought I should devote much more time to a more extensive review of his presidency, and see if this happened to be a case where a president didn't receive the credit that was properly due him. I thought that with the perspective of almost a quarter century, perhaps Carter's term in office could be better appreciated, as was Truman's long after he left office.

To put it mildly, Carter's sheer volume of achievements, both in and out of the White House, absolutely amazed me when I began listing one after the other. Those achievements, in tandem with Carter's remarkable poll-leading position in the unscientific survey I conducted, are what served as the motivation for publishing the book, while his heroic actions in Haiti became the inspiration for *Welcome Back, Carter.* Granted, there's always the chance that my polling may have produced the most delusional results since a poll of *Literary Digest* readers in 1936 forecast a landslide for Kansas Governor Alf Landon over FDR. But I don't think that's the case here. So despite not having any stature as an average citizen, and no experience as a professional pollster, I chose to publish my survey results and my compilation of the Carter record and see whether or not my first-place Carter ranking could be verified by one or more of the professional polling organizations.

Welcome Back, Carter isn't the most appropriate title for this book, because it implies he only recently has regained favor with a large segment of the American public, specifically for his winning the Nobel Peace Prize in 2002. Nothing could be further from the truth; polls as early as 1986 showed him with a majority positive rating, as his activities with the Carter Center and Habitat for Humanity were widely applauded. While he long ago regained the esteem of the nation, my informal poll indicates that he has come back in the hearts and minds of a substantial number of voters as their preferred candidate for the 2004 Democratic nomination. If these numbers are verified by respected polling companies as having merit, it's easy to see Carter being asked by the media about the poll results and whether he could be compelled to consider a run for a second term. Of course, if he categorically ruled out such an attempt, then, the question would be put to rest. I've become more and more convinced that news of his declining to run would be greeted with relief by the Republican Party, which would have avoided the daunting task of possibly facing an enormously respected former president of the United States, one whose policy positions are the results of long-held convictions (which is seen also by many as the chief characteristic about President Bush that Americans admire in the wake of September 11, 2001). Because of their contrasting firm beliefs, I feel a Bush-Carter contest would provide one of the clearest distinctions in philosophies in presidential election history. And while I can't prove it, in my estimation the excitement of a Bush-Carter race would raise voter turnout to levels not seen since the JFK-Nixon contest in 1960.

ONE

BELIEVE IT: CARTER WINS THE POLL

I've been fascinated with politics since November of 1972, which can be illustrated by events from my scholastic career. One of my sixth-grade teachers conducted a straw poll just prior to election day that resulted in the Nixon-Agnew ticket routing McGovern-Shriver by a vote of 24 to 1, which, it turned out, accurately previewed the ensuing Republican landslide. I can also clearly recall a social studies class assignment in the fall of 1976 that required us to make campaign signs for either Ford or Carter (mine was "Don't Go Nuts; Vote Ford"), and in college in 1980, I remember having to critique the Reagan-Carter debate as an extra credit project for my U.S. history class. It turned out that I'd overestimated the importance in a presidential debate of having command of the facts, which was Carter's strength, and underestimated the value of Reagan's reassuring manner and timely one-liners, in this case, "There you go again," which many political commentators deemed a Reagan knockout blow. Indeed, within a few days, what had been a close race turned into a Republican landslide.

And in 1984, my alma mater's speakers program brought in George McGovern to lecture on the eve of the Mondale-Reagan election. Reagan guaranteed himself an easy re-election, said McGovern, when he put the age issue to rest (after a poor first debate against Mondale) when he made even Mondale laugh by saying in their second debate, "I will not make age an issue in this campaign; I will not exploit, for political purposes, my opponent's youth and inexperience." When I asked McGovern for an autograph after his speech, I confessed to having taken one of my Dad's lighters to school and during recess giving a hotfoot to the kid in my sixth-grade gym class who had boasted at having cast the only Democratic vote in our straw poll; my classmate in turn defended himself by spraying me with a hose that he unscrewed from one of the sprinklers on the school soccer field. McGovern laughed at that, saying he appreciated the support of anyone who was in agreement with his philosophy that, "You don't fight fire with fire— you fight fire with water!"

A few years after graduating from college, I landed a job that has kept me on the road for roughly four months annually but has enabled me to meet a diverse cross-section of America. During my travels through the country since 1988, I've entertained myself every election cycle by conducting impromptu one-on-one polls with people from all walks of life, such as industry leaders, middle management types, soccer moms, cab drivers, butchers, bellmen, retirees and young adults voting in their first election. My motive for doing these field surveys was sheer curiosity, to see how my unscientific sampling would compare to the professional pollsters during each campaign and then to chart my numbers with the actual post-election vote totals.

I learned years ago about a revealing polling story from the 1948 election, which had been continually forecast as an easy victory for Republican challenger Thomas Dewey over President Truman. The Staley Milling Company, a midwestern business which specialized in chicken feed, offered its customers a choice of feed sacks that were emblazoned DEMOCRAT or REPUBLICAN. The company disbanded its experiment two months before the election with the Democrats holding a comfortable lead, dismissing the results as a certain fluke. I believe that farmer's survey illustrated that conventional wisdom can sometimes best be challenged by unconventional methods.

As noted earlier, instead of waiting to poll the 2004 general election race in the summer and fall of that year between President Bush and the Democratic nominee, I thought I'd test the waters much earlier than usual and solicit opinions from Democrats and independent swing voters in early 2003 about the declared contenders for the Democratic nomination. In an almost eerie replay of the 2000 election, of the exactly 300 politically aware people who allowed me to question them initially (roughly 500 others declined to participate, saying they weren't yet aware who was running and wouldn't start paying attention until much later in the year), 106 called themselves Republicans (I excluded Republicans from this Democratic polling exercise), 112 claimed to be Democrats, and 85 stated they were independent. Missouri Congressman Richard Gephardt led the Democratic field with 21% of the vote, just ahead of former Vermont Governor Howard Dean at 19%, with Connecticut Senator Joe Lieberman at 14%, Massachusetts Senator John Kerry garnered 13%, Florida Senator Bob

Graham drew 4%, and North Carolina Senator John Edwards 3%; none of the other candidates finished higher than 1%, while the undecideds amounted to 23% (retired General Wesley Clark didn't enter the race until long after this poll).

I noticed how my survey mirrored national polls of a professional variety—keeping in mind that while Dean led in Iowa and New Hampshire, he wasn't leading nationally—so there was nothing out of the ordinary in my results. Nor was it surprising to hear the comments of many of those undecideds when I asked them if they preferred either of the two highest profile Democrats on the sidelines, New York Senator Hillary Clinton and former Vice President Al Gore. Clinton was the favorite of nearly one-third (30%) of the undecided vote, while Gore received 13%. The numbers on Clinton and Gore were also fairly compatible with other polls I've seen regarding a hypothetical candidacy by either one of them.

But what did surprise me greatly were the number of undecideds who *volunteered* how their first choice would actually be Jimmy Carter, if he ever decided to attempt a comeback for the ages and seek a second term nearly a quarter century after being turned out of office in a landslide to Ronald Reagan. Granted, only 11% of the undecided vote expressed a preference for Carter, but I thought that number was significant, considering his name wasn't included in my list of candidates, not to mention his 11% was just 2% less than the man who finished with approximately a half million more votes than George W. Bush in the 2000 election.

Among the remarks made on Carter's behalf were, "He has incredible stature, much more than any living Democrat," "His prestige is unmatched," "His compassion for people is authentic beyond question," "He was unfairly blamed for the recession he inherited, which was ignited when OPEC tripled fuel prices," and "He could've played golf and settled into an easy retirement, but instead became a champion for peace and one of the world's greatest humanitarians." And on it went.

Having received all the unexpected Carter feedback, I began to wonder about his potential support if his name was *included among the candidates* in the announced Democratic field. I spent the next 3 months speaking to an additional 300 citizens (with perhaps double that number declining once again due to lack of interest or familiarity with the candidates, or maybe because they thought I was trying to sell them something); of those 300, 116 claimed to be Democrats, 109 said they were Republicans, and 76 indicated they were independents (again, I did not solicit opinions from the 109 Republicans I met during this sampling). Even though I included Carter's name on the list with all the announced candidates, I felt justified in leaving off the names of Clinton and Gore, since they had stated unequivocally that they were not going to run in 2004. Although many Carter backers were skeptical that he would ever agree to run, for the sake of my unscientific poll, I asked them to assume he would run if public opinion convinced him he had solid support of Democrats and swing voters. The results were convincing: Carter 26%, Kerry 15%, Gephardt 14%, Dean 14%, Lieberman 11%, Edwards 5%, Graham 3%, with the remaining candidates coming in at under 1% and the undecideds at 9%.

I attributed much of Carter's vote to name recognition, of course, but still found myself amazed by the level of his support, even if by professional polling standards my relatively small sample size was statistically insignificant. I was nonetheless tempted to forward these results to the Carter Center in Atlanta, but I disposed of the notion because of three logical reasons. First, like those skeptics mentioned above, I was certain because of his age that he'd never even entertain the idea of running, to say nothing of actually declaring himself a candidate for the Democratic nomination. Second, I considered the worldwide niche he's carved out for himself with the Carter Center; the man appears to be *too busy* to seek re-election. And third, as all married men know, there are certain things a husband shouldn't do without first receiving approval from his wife, and I think somewhere high on that list would be running for president of the United States. Even if Carter would consider it an honor to run for the presidency, I knew those thoughts would be rendered moot once Rosalynn Carter vetoed the idea of his seeking re-election, which she undoubtedly would.

So, my project completed, I let things go at that; I felt like a fisherman who spends his spare time reeling in bass from sunup to sundown, only to throw them all back. The results were secondary to the action—and it wasn't a bad way to meet several hundred people over the course of four months. For me it has always been a fun way to spend 15 minutes a day and alleviate the boredom that comes with down time while away from home on business.

Although I'd decided to dispose the Carter matter from my mind, on occasion I'd see a complimentary story about his winning the Nobel Peace Prize, or hear mention of a national poll that voted him the second-most admired American (behind President Bush). Or I'd read his editorial that appeared in USA TODAY and the New York Times that forcefully came out against the forthcoming war against Iraq, calling it an unjust war to due a lack of evidence that Iraq posed an imminent threat to the United States, while seriously questioning the Bush Administration's assertion that Iraq still possessed weapons of mass destruction.

The more I reflected on these events, the less reason I saw to disbelieve those survey results that saw Carter top the Democratic field. The American people trusted him, even if they didn't always agree with him, and knew that his integrity was unassailable. He'd dedicated his life to waging peace, improving health, and building hope around the world. His age didn't seem all that relevant anymore; he just didn't seem to slow down. And it occurred to me that there was past evidence that the American public doesn't automatically rule out a candidate because of advanced age. President Reagan could have very likely won a third term if 1988, if he wasn't prohibited by the 22nd Amendment, even though he was approaching 80 himself.

Yet whenever I thought about forwarding my informal poll results to the Carter Center, in the remote event that he'd be compelled to at least entertain the thought of seeking the Democratic nomination in 2004, I kept coming back to the one factor that made all this a pipedream: he wouldn't seek re-election without the support of his full-time partner of over a half-century, and of course the former First Lady would dismiss the idea out of hand and tell her husband that if he had all this energy, that there would always be more conflicts he could mediate, more elections to monitor around the world, more speeches he could give on behalf of human rights, more countries in Africa that needed diseases to be eradicated, and more homes they could build for Habitat for Humanity. Of course she wouldn't let him run.

I spent part of a summer evening in 2003 away from home reviewing some old articles about Carter on the Internet. One story, with the byline of CBS News.com, was written in July of 2002, and it touched upon the varied activities of the former president, including his recent visit to Cuba, where he gave a sharply critical and uncensored speech to Cuban citizens, criticizing their nation's human rights record, but at the same time calling for an end to the American trade embargo with Cuba and a restoration of diplomatic relations with the Castro government. Then, for the first time that I'd ever seen in print, Rosalynn Carter was asked if she ever wanted to return to the White House as a resident. Her thoughts on a second Carter Administration? "I would love for him to be president again…"

Shows what I know. If Rosalynn was for the idea, then the only one could rule out a possible Carter candidacy was Carter himself. Yet when I read one of his comments in the story, I became convinced the former president *could* be compelled to consider running, when he said, "I have no ambition to be president again." When reading between the lines, it's easy to decipher that his saying he had "no ambition" was hardly a Shermanesque decline ("I will not run if nominated; I will not serve if elected"). The problem, of course, was that he had no knowledge of the depth of support I would later discover from Democrats and independents, and without any solid numbers with which he could justify seeking the Democratic nomination, there would be no reason for him to give the matter any thought.

Still, before I did anything else, I paused for a few weeks of reappraisal, in the manner of writing a letter and then sticking it in a drawer to allow one's self the opportunity to view it more objectively with the passage of time. I finally determined that the underlying reason for my hesitation was that while I had a general idea of his successes and setbacks as president and a basic knowledge of his accomplishments since leaving office, I hardly considered myself well-versed on either subject. I decided to review the

Carter record of the last quarter century, working backwards from his post-presidency to his term in office, and weigh his career in the balance.

Although his achievements since leaving Washington have been well chronicled, I was still taken aback about the breadth of accomplishments he'd experienced in his post-presidency, once all the material was amassed before me. I saw no reason to devote an inordinate amount of detail on his works since leaving the White House, since a widespread consensus emerged in the 1990s which recognized Carter as the greatest former president in our history; with that case already having been made to the public, I thought it would be wiser to chronicle a lengthier review of his presidency through the prism of nearly 25 years, and to ascertain whether any of his administration's achievements had been overshadowed by an OPEC-sparked recession and the Iran hostage crisis. After all, it took roughly two decades for Truman's administration to be re-appraised in a positive fashion, and I wondered if it Carter's record as president could also be viewed in a better light a generation after leaving office. To my surprise, when itemizing his specific actions as president, I came away convinced that his record was severely underestimated while he was in office, in the manner of Truman's, which seems to be the fate of visionaries who appear on the scene ahead of their time. Before addressing Carter's presidency, however, I will touch upon his post-presidential achievements with the Carter Center.

TWO

WAGING PEACE

President Carter's reputation gives the Carter Center Peace Programs the credibility needed to work nationally, regionally, and globally.

The achievements of President Carter's Peace Programs include the:

- Americas Program to improve the quality of democracy, thwart corruption, decrease social inequities, and reduce trade barriers in the Western Hemisphere
- Conflict Resolution Program to prevent and resolve armed and political conflicts around the globe
- Democracy Program to work worldwide for the development of democratic societies as the best way to promote human rights, achieve sustainable economic development, and resolve conflicts peacefully, and the

- Global Development Initiative to assist developing countries with the expertise to help them devise their own plans for sustainable development.

Whether the Carter Center is working on anti-corruption efforts in Latin America, conflict resolution in Sudan, a national development strategy in Guyana, or with civil society groups in Peru or Zambia, the end result is the empowerment of people. The Carter Center's work creates long-term effects by laying and strengthening frameworks within a country's institutions, whether it's through the electoral commission, judicial circuit, or a network of nongovernmental organizations seeking a voice in the national agenda.

CARTER CENTER PEACE INITIATIVES

- Observing elections in emerging democracies or those in danger of backsliding from democracy
- Seeking an end to the civil war in Sudan
- Mediating peaceful transfers of authority in contested elections
- Promoting inter-American relations and democratic accountability
- Strengthening the capacity of civic organizations to participate in government policy making and promoting the rule of law
- Advocating for stronger international human rights systems and help new democracies establish human rights laws and institutions

- Promoting sustainable development through comprehensive country-specific strategies.

AMERICAS PROGRAM

The Carter Center established the Americas Program in 1986, when the Western Hemisphere was undergoing dramatic political changes, striving toward democracy and opening economies. The program, a pioneer in monitoring elections, made important contributions to these profound changes in the region.

Today, the program helps deepen inter-American relations through high-level policy conferences on hemispheric issues. The initial emphasis on promoting democracy through elections has evolved into second-generation projects to ensure new democracies are meaningful in everyday life. Striving to make governments more accountable, the program helps citizens and governments fight corruption, develop methods to make political financing more transparent, and involve civic groups in public dialogue with governments on crucial national issues and laws.

The Council of Presidents and Prime Ministers of the Americas is key to these efforts. Based at the Americas Program, the Council includes more than 35 current and former leaders from the Western Hemisphere led by President Carter. The Council uses its experience and voice to give visibility to pressing issues, search for cooperative solutions to problems, bring together divided countries, and promote policy reform and concrete action by multilateral organizations, governments, the private sector, and nongovernmental organizations.

INTER-AMERICAN RELATIONS

Countries throughout the Western Hemisphere struggle with an interrelated set of issues from debt, drugs, and deforestation to weak democracies. Many of these issues have both domestic and international components and can only be resolved through cooperative approaches involving several countries. Building on the findings of action-oriented conferences, the Americas Program has helped create coalitions to support stronger regional protection of democracy and implementation of the hemispheric anticorruption treaty.

- At the Summit of the Americas in Quebec in March 2001, the Council of Presidents and Prime Ministers of the Americas urged the successful adoption of a clause requiring countries to maintain competitive elections and democratic standards to participate in future summits and in the Free Trade Area of the Americas.
- The program also provided expert advice on the subsequent Inter-American Democracy Charter, adopted by the Organization of American States in September 2001.

The program explored ways to move toward normal relations between the United States and Cuba. President Carter visited Cuba in May 2002—the first sitting or former U.S. president to do so since 1928. He called on the U.S. administration to end the trade embargo against Cuba and for Cuba to allow for elections and more civil liberties.

DEMOCRATIC ACCOUNTABILITY

The Americas Program helps foster democracy and build accountability by promoting open, transparent interaction and communication between citizens and their government leaders, as well as by strengthening systems of accountability within and between government agencies. The program strengthens the citizen voice by promoting free and fair elections, broadening access to information so citizens can monitor government performance, fostering public discussion of proposed legislation, and encouraging routine publication of government documents—a crucial element of the people's "right to know" in a democracy.

The program took a leading role in the Center's monitoring of elections in Peru (2000 and 2001), Jamaica (2002), and Nicaragua (2001). The lead-up to the November 2001 elections in Nicaragua created serious concern in the international community that poor-quality elections could further diminish confidence in the electoral branch of government. The Center, in its report on the elections, highlighted the erosion of accountability in state institutions.

- The program took a leading role in the Center's monitoring of elections in Peru (2000 and 2001), Jamaica (2002), and Nicaragua (2001). The lead-up to the November 2001 elections in Nicaragua created serious concern in the international community that poor-quality elections could further diminish confidence in the electoral branch of government. The Center, in its report on the elections, highlighted the erosion of accountability in state institutions.

- Reaching out to enlightened corporate citizens, the Center's Council for Ethical Business Practices brings together top Atlanta business people to share their experiences with corporate codes of conduct and enforcement of the Foreign Corrupt Practices Act, generating insights about how to deal with the realities of corruption while doing business abroad.

- After monitoring the 1998 and 2000 elections and the process of writing a new constitution in 1999, the program coordinated a symposium in 2001 in Caracas on Venezuela's elections and political future that helped identify weaknesses in its democratic practices. In response to the short-lived removal of President Hugo Chavez from power in April 2002, the program led the Center's involvement in promoting national reconciliation in Venezuela, in partnership with the OAS and UNDP.

CONFLICT RESOLUTION PROGRAM

Ending suffering and building sustainable peace are key goals of the Carter Center's Conflict Resolution Program. The program monitors many of the world's armed conflicts in an attempt to better understand their histories, the primary actors involved, disputed issues, and efforts being made to resolve them.

Peace takes more than an end to fighting. The underlying causes of violent conflict must be addressed to prevent its resurgence. As a nonpartisan, nongovernmental organization with access to world leaders and expertise in mediation, negotiation, and peacebuilding, the Center helps warring parties when traditional dispute resolution methods are not effective. Governments follow "track one," or official diplomacy, while nongovernmental organizations typically pursue "track two," or unofficial diplomatic activities that directly impact the people most affected by the conflict. The Carter Center can be termed a "track 1.5" organization because it occupies a special place, a nongovernmental organization with unique access to track one levels. It can also operate in a more classical track two role, engaging in longer-term peace-building activities.

To resolve conflicts, the Center coordinates its efforts with those of other nongovernmental organizations, intergovernmental organizations, and governments. The program holds consultations with organizations to avoid duplication of efforts or contradictory plans and to increase the positive effects of conflict resolution work.

The program also is the base for the International Council for Conflict Resolution, a small body of internationally recognized experts in mediating conflict and promoting peace and who can offer advice and assistance in resolving disputes. These experts play an important role in advising the efforts of CRP and will be engaged on an individual basis in ongoing CRP projects. In autumn 2002, the ICCR convened to address longstanding conflicts in the Middle East and Kashmir. ICCR sent its recommendations for prospective diplomatic strategies to interested governments and international organizations.

NEGOTIATION, MEDIATION, AND PEACE IMPLEMENTATION

The Carter Center and the Conflict Resolution Program have a worldwide reputation based on their record of achievements in direct negotiations and mediations at the highest levels. Often when a peace accord is reached, there is a collective sigh of relief. But an end to fighting is by no means the end of the road. The sometimes protracted processes that lead to a peace agreement represent the beginning of an even longer process of peace implementation and reconciliation.

- One recent example is the Conflict Resolution Program's work in Sudan and in Uganda. The most recent phase of Sudan's civil war has ravaged the country for the past 18 years, killing two million people and displacing four million. Sudan's southern neighbor, Uganda, has faced its own long-term insurgency from the Lord's Resistance Army. In this complex environment, relations between Sudan and Uganda foundered based on allegations of support by the governments for rebels fighting in each other's countries.

- The Conflict Resolution Program was invited in 1999 by the Ugandan and Sudanese governments to address the conflict in northern Uganda and improve their deteriorating relationship. The result was the Nairobi Agreement of December 1999, brokered by President Carter and signed by the two presidents.

- Since then, the program has worked intensively to help implement the agreement, convening numerous meetings between the two countries, other interested parties, and rebel leaders deep in the bush of southern Sudan.

- Despite a resurgence of fighting in northern Uganda in early 2002, the program has been instrumental in the return of 300 abducted women and children from the LRA to their homes in Uganda and in the exchange of all prisoners of war. Sudan and

17

Uganda also have resumed diplomatic relations, an important step in achieving regional peace.

- In 2002, the program helped foster international support for a revitalized peace effort in Sudan and trained senior government and rebel leaders in negotiating skills and mediation techniques. The program provided advice to the Inter-Governmental Authority on Development, the East African body that convened Sudan peace talks. President Carter continues to travel to the region and remains closely in touch with key leaders.

- Since 1991, the Center has worked to bring peace and democracy to Liberia by engaging interim governments and faction leaders. Although the Center closed its field office in 2000, dissatisfied with the government's behavior, the Center has continued to reconcile President Charles Taylor and opposition parties. The program advised and guided mediation strategies at the Economic Community of West Africa States sponsored meetings in Abuja in 2002, aimed at advancing reconciliation between the government and opposition.

- In 1994, President Carter, along with Colin Powell and Sam Nunn, went to Haiti, where they negotiated an agreement that peacefully removed military leader Gen. Raoul Cedras from power and thus negated the need for armed intervention by the U.S. Army.

VIOLENCE PREVENTION, PEACE BUILDING, AND RECONCILIATION

Preventing armed conflict in volatile atmospheres is a critical challenge. Parties in dispute sometimes seek a neutral third party to facilitate dialogue to avert conflict. Peacebuilding and reconciliation, which will be required long after the end of violent conflict, demands patient, persistent efforts to bring former combatants together to forge a shared future.

- In Venezuela, the Conflict Resolution Program and the Americas Program are working to advance dialogue between the government and the opposition. After a failed coup in April 2002, President Hugo Chavez's opposition organized a mass demonstration, denouncing what they believe his authoritarian populism. The Center is providing technical guidance and mediation techniques on conflict resolution.
- In Guyana, deep divisions along ethnic lines have stymied Guyana's political and economic development and led to increased violence. In June 2002, the program led a workshop on conflict prevention techniques and conflict analysis for leaders of Guyana's business, legal, and religious communities and of nongovernmental organizations.

OTHER EFFORTS WORLDWIDE

- At the request of Bosnian Serb leader Radovan Karadzic and with the approval of President Clinton in December 1994,

19

President and Mrs. Carter and two Center staff members brokered the terms of a four-month cease-fire in Bosnia and a pledge from all sides to resume peace talks. President Carter later testified before the Senate, urging U.S. influence be used to bring the factions back to the negotiating table. A peace agreement was reached in 1995 during U.S.-sponsored talks in Dayton, Ohio.

- After North Korea withdrew its membership in the International Atomic Energy Agency and threatened to expel the agency's inspectors, the United States began pushing for U.N. sanctions, fearing North Korea was developing an atomic arsenal. At the invitation from President Kim Il Sung, President and Mrs. Carter traveled to North Korea, and after talks, President Kim agreed to freeze its nuclear program in exchange for resumption of a dialogue with the United States. The ensuing dialogue was the first between the countries in 40 years and resulted in North Korea's promise to significantly change some nuclear energy production facilities.

- The Carter Center brought together heads of state from Burundi, Rwanda, Tanzania, Uganda and Zaire, collectively known as the Great Lakes region of Africa, during summits in Cairo in 1995 and Tunis in 1996 to address violence in the region and the need to repatriate 1.7 million Rwandan refugees living in Zaire. The leaders agreed on several actions to start to bring peace, reconciliation, and development to their troubled region.

- Invited by Ecuador President Gustavo Noboa and in partnership with the Center's Americas Program, the Conflict Resolution

Program designed a long-term plan in 2000 to bridge the ethnic and political divisions within the country. The Center brought together members of the three largest indigenous advocacy groups to help design a plan to work more productively with the government on their causes.

The program worked in Estonia to ease tensions over citizenship and language issues by holding workshops for parties to work through their differences. The program's Baltics project led the Estonians to welcome the Russians to their parliament sessions and to collaborate on new joint projects.

DEMOCRACY PROGRAMS

The Democracy Program works in three principal ways: conducting international election monitoring; strengthening the capacity of civic organizations to participate in government policy making; and promoting the rule of law. In all of its work, the Democracy Program incorporates a commitment to the protection and advancement of human rights values, upon which President Carter and Rosalynn Carter founded the Carter Center.

The Center believes people can improve their lives when they are empowered to exercise control over how they are governed. The Democracy Program works with other Carter Center programs, such as the Global Development Initiative and the Conflict Resolution Program, to realize this goal. The involvement of other Center programs creates the comprehensive, long-term strategic approach needed to help nations build peaceful, just, and economically viable societies.

OBSERVING ELECTIONS AROUND THE WORLD

Effective election monitoring begins long before voters cast their ballots. The Carter Center requires an invitation from the country's electoral authorities and a welcome from the major political parties to ensure the Center can play a meaningful nonpartisan role. Observers analyze election laws, assess voter registration processes, voter education efforts, and the openness of campaigns, focusing on competitiveness, unhindered participation in the election process, and access to the media. These assessments begin months in advance. The presence of impartial observers reassures voters they can safely and secretly cast their ballots and that vote tabulation will be conducted without tampering. Thus, election monitoring deters interference or fraud in the voting process. The Carter Center has observed more than 40 elections in 21 countries on four continents:

- Sierra Leone held presidential and parliamentary elections in May 2002 following the end of a 10-year civil war. The Carter Center was the only U.S. based organization that monitored the elections, which observers found were peaceful and relatively well managed. The delegation commended the voters of Sierra Leone, political party agents, and polling station workers for their impressive commitment to peaceful voting under very challenging conditions. The Carter Center noted the need for increased transparency in election rules and decisions by the

Election Commission and improved voter registration process and voter education.

- In support of democratic development in Mali and the rest of West Africa, the Center observed both rounds of Mali's 2002 presidential elections. Overall, the Carter Center found the elections characterized by a peaceful, tolerant, and competitive political climate, although both rounds were characterized by widespread procedural irregularities. Perhaps most importantly, the winning candidate, Amadou Toumani Touré, appears to enjoy legitimacy in the eyes of the Malian electorate and the international community.

- Observing its third election in East Timor since 1999, the Carter Center commended the new country on its presidential election that met international standards for freeness and fairness. The Center monitored the violent 1999 referendum vote for independence from Indonesia and the 2001 vote for the Constituent Assembly. In its statement, the Center said democratic development would be needed at all levels of government if East Timor is to succeed as a democratic nation.

- The Center lauded the large and peaceful turnout in Zambia's presidential and parliamentary elections in December 2001. The Center's delegation, co-led by former Nigeria Head of State Abdulsalami Abubakar, former Benin President Nicéphore Soglo, and former Tanzania Prime Minister Judge Joseph Warioba, also reported vote-counting procedures sometimes were chaotic and tabulation of results in constituency centers and at the Electoral Commission was not fully transparent. The governing party candidate, Levy Mwanawasa, won just 29 percent of the vote and narrowly defeated a divided opposition, which lodged claims of vote rigging.

STRENGTHENING CIVIL SOCIETY

The Center works to strengthen the capabilities of nongovernmental civic organizations so that citizens have a clear avenue to participate fully in the political process. A politically active civil society plays a critical role in deepening democratic institutions, but in most emerging democracies these civic organizations lack full working knowledge of democratic principles and human rights standards. The Center trains media in the responsibilities of a free press, facilitates dialogue and reconciliation among competing national groups, and provides useful working tools to improve the effectiveness of human rights monitors and advocates. Priority is given to supporting the political participation of traditionally marginalized segments of society, such as women, indigenous peoples, refugees, and youth.

Following its observation of Zambia's contentious elections in December 2001, the program worked with civil society groups and newly elected national legislators to improve their working relationships and channels of communication.

- Before East Timor's first presidential election in April 2002 since gaining independence, the Center helped local communities evaluate programs to improve relations between police and citizens.

- The program has worked in Guyana since 2000 to strengthen civil society, thus helping the country overcome conflictive ethnic divisions. With training from the Center, local civic organizations focusing on women, youth and Amerindians are increasing their advocacy and participation in public policy.

- After the civil war in Liberia ended in 1997, the Democracy Program worked with the government and civil society organizations to help strengthen democratic institutions. The Center trained human rights monitors and paralegals, held workshops on incorporating human rights principles into school curricula, and trained media in the roles and responsibilities of a free press.

STRENGTHENING RULE OF LAW

Sustainable democratic governance depends upon a legal system that protects people's individual rights and property. The judicial system must enjoy public confidence and be seen to resolve disputes efficiently and administer justice fairly. Many countries in transition from authoritarian rule are plagued by corrupt or inefficient judicial systems. The program is enhancing the expertise of judges, court personnel, and lawyers in Guyana, a young democracy. Activities with the bar association and legal aid groups are informing citizens of their rights under the law. New court rules and procedures and a new code of ethics have been drafted through working groups of concerned citizens, also a demonstration of the important role of civil society.

PROTECTING HUMAN RIGHTS

One of the founding principles of the Carter Center is a commitment to human rights. The Center advocates for stronger international human rights systems, sends human rights monitors on election observation missions, helps new democracies establish human rights laws and institutions, and intervenes on behalf of victims of human rights abuses. Under the auspices of the Democracy Program, the Center's initiatives are supervised by a human rights attorney and are accomplished by staff in each of the Center's programs.

National institutions and laws protecting human rights are essential to deepening democracy. The Democracy Program helps emerging democracies incorporate human rights precepts into institutions, such as human rights commissions, educational systems, and the judiciary. Staff have provided training to police officials, judges and lawyers, the media, and local nongovernmental organizations and have reported on human rights issues during election observation missions in Nigeria, Indonesia, East Timor, and Sierra Leone.

Strengthening the international human rights system also contributes to democratic transitions around the world by setting and enforcing standards for governments' behavior toward individuals and groups. For example, the Center held a series of four consultations with the United Nations Office of the High Commissioner for Human Rights to define the office's mandate and to improve coordination among various parts of the United Nations' human rights program, such as U.N. human rights offices and human rights investigators.

GLOBAL DEVELOPMENT INITIATIVE

Bridging the unacceptable gap between the rich and the poor of our world is the greatest challenge of our time. The Carter Center therefore views global development not only to be a moral concern, but also imperative to achieving world peace. To this end, development cooperation is critical and can be effective only where sound policies are nationally owned, where people have the capacity to determine such policies, where enabling resources are made available, and where the donor community effectively coordinates in support of a country's national strategy.

At the end of the Cold War, wealthy, developed countries turned their backs on developing countries when they most needed support. Aid from international agencies often was given to promote an international agenda and conditions were placed on countries that they could not meet or that did not address their own priorities and needs. Meanwhile, developing countries took a top-down approach to economic and social policies because they lacked many of the democratic institutions that permit citizens and citizens' groups to participate in public decisions and promote government accountability and transparency. These governments also often lacked the capacity to manage foreign aid coming from multiple sources, resulting in duplicated efforts, wasted resources, and inappropriate projects. The Global Development Initiative is an integral part of the Carter Center's Peace Programs. It promotes a new model of development cooperation based upon three core principles:

- Greater country ownership of development strategies;
- Increased participation of civil society in governance and policymaking; and
- Effective international partnership and cooperation.

These principles are advanced through on-the-ground work in four partner countries and through a series of periodic, high-level Development Cooperation Forums to draw lessons from the country experiences and examine the impact that global forces and policies are having on the development of poor countries. Albania, Guyana, Mali, and Mozambique are the initiative's current partner countries. The initiative is working in its partner countries with the government, private sector, civil society, and international donors to help devise country-owned strategies for sustainable development and democracy.

The Global Development Initiative brings unique assets to these efforts. The Carter Center is neutral and has a proven track record of successfully bringing diverse stakeholders together on difficult issues to ensure participation and ownership. The Center can convene high-level officials to influence change and take action to improve global development policies and practices. Together, these capacities place the Global Development Initiative in a special position to enhance global development cooperation and facilitate the formulation of national development strategies.

A NATIONAL DEVELOPMENT STRATEGY

Recognizing that effective change cannot be promoted from outside a country, but must spring from within, many developing countries and international development institutions have begun promoting the concept of a National Development Strategy.

A National Development Strategy outlines a broad vision for the transformation of a society and the essential policies, investments, and actions that need to be taken by the business community, governments, nongovernmental organizations and individual citizens to make it happen. The process of developing a strategy is crucial: it must be participatory and include all elements of society. Participation is crucial to managing change and to developing a more democratic culture where governments listen to people and people take ownership of decisions.

After an invitation from a government, the Global Development Initiative works with civil society leaders, business leaders, and representatives of nongovernmental organizations to organize and manage a process to create a National Development Strategy. This process includes gathering and disseminating information, training local groups in policy analysis, conducting 'town hall' style meetings throughout the country, researching and debating alternative public policies, holding meetings between government officials and nongovernmental organizations to jointly craft proposals, and promoting debate of issues among elected representatives. A National Development Strategy process is usually led by a steering group of eminent civic, business, and political leaders.

This broad-based participation is crucial to fostering sustainable development. Such collaboration is likely to result in better, more appropriate development policies because they are based on the knowledge and experience of those most affected by poverty and underdevelopment. The National Development Strategy process strengthens democracy and respect for all aspects of human rights by reinforcing democratic institutions and supporting a more participatory, cooperative, and democratically inclusive culture. When citizens have a greater stake in formulating their national strategy, they view their democratic institutions with a greater sense of legitimacy.

The Center has been invited to support national development strategy efforts in four countries. Since each country's political, economic, and social circumstances are different, and each is at a different stage of development, the National Development Strategy process in each country differs, but adheres to the basic principles of the Global Development Initiative.

- The Carter Center has worked in Guyana for more than a decade to help the country overcome deep ethnic divisions and rebuild its economy. The initiative brought together more than 200 Guyanese experts from the business community, labor unions, and nongovernmental organizations to help draft the National Development Strategy, which addressed more than 20 major sectors of society. The initiative continues to work with all the actors to promote the adoption and implementation of the strategy.

- The Global Development Initiative is working with the government of Albania and citizens' groups to advance the country's Growth and Poverty Reduction Strategy. The Global Development Initiative facilitated unprecedented collaboration between government, nongovernmental organizations, and citizens in the GPRS process by disseminating information about the process, supporting public access to research, strengthening nongovernmental organizations' capacity to analyze policy, organizing "town hall" meetings throughout the country, and bringing government officials and nongovernmental organizations together in working groups to develop strategies and policy options. The Carter Center will help to forge consensus around Albania's long-term priorities, establish and train networks of civil society groups around the country to participate more actively in the policymaking process, and promote greater international cooperation around Albania's national objectives.

- The government of Mali invited the Center to work with civil society and the government to strengthen the institutions needed to establish realistic, integrated development priorities in a participatory manner; improve government coordination of development policies, programs, and projects; and build the government's capacity to coordinate the international aid system in Mali.

THE DEVELOPMENT COOPERATION FORUM SERIES

Periodically, the Global Development Initiative convenes a high-level, international Development Cooperation Forum. The forums convene leading thinkers and practitioners to take stock of the current state of development cooperation, identify ways in which such cooperation can be promoted more effectively, and reflect on future challenges to these endeavors. The Initiative's work with its partner countries serves as the practical basis of discussions.

SUMMARIES OF PAST DEVELOPMENT COOPERATION FORUMS:

First Forum: Chaired by President Carter and U.N. Secretary General Boutros Boutros-Ghali in a hopeful atmosphere for development following the end of the Cold War, the Global Development Cooperation forum of 1992 examined specific and practical ways to improve development cooperation on an international scale. Following the conference, the Center convened an action-planning meeting of experts, donor officials, and country representatives that led to the establishment of the Global Development Initiative.

Second Forum: Chaired by President Carter and attended by the president, finance minister, and opposition leader of Guyana as well as development ministers, aid agency representatives, and leaders from the private sector and civil society, the 1996 forum reviewed the results of the initiative's efforts in Guyana to facilitate the participatory preparation of a National Development Strategy. Participants at the meetings called the Guyana effort a potential new model of development cooperation emphasizing the principles of ownership, participation, and international partnership. The Center was encouraged at the meeting to expand its country-based initiatives to Africa.

Third Forum: Chaired by President Carter and former U.S. Treasury Secretary Robert Rubin, the 2002 forum was convened to take stock of a decade of reforms in development cooperation and examine the impact of these reforms on the program's four partner countries - Albania, Guyana, Mali, and Mozambique. The 2002 forum took place a month ahead of the

International Conference on Financing for Development in Monterrey, Mexico. President Carter took the messages of the 2002 Forum to Monterrey and added his voice to those calling for greater generosity from donor countries to achieve the Millennium Development Goals.

Fourth Forum: The next Development Cooperation Forum is planned for mid-2004. The Global Development Initiative and its partners will analyze the progress achieved since the last forum in the production and implementation of National Development Strategies with particular attention to how the Monterrey Consensus and the Millennium Development Goals may or may not have contributed to progress.

HUMAN RIGHTS INITIATIVES

In his Nobel Peace Prize acceptance statement, President Carter said: "My concept of human rights has grown to include not only the right to live in peace, but also to adequate health care, shelter, food, and to economic opportunity. I hope this award reflects a universal acceptance and even embrace of this broad-based concept of human rights."

The commitment to human rights is one of the founding principles of the Carter Center, and the Center undertakes a range of activities to promote human rights around the world:

- Strengthening international human rights systems through expert consultations and advocacy with heads of state and the United Nations
- Intervening on behalf of human rights abuses

- Including human rights monitoring as part of election observation missions and other international delegations, and

- Integrating human rights approaches and principles into the activities of all Carter Center programs.

The Center's key activities include the following:

- President and Mrs. Carter intervene on behalf of human rights victims around the world. President and Mrs. Carter often take their human rights concerns to heads of states in personal meetings and through letters. The Carters use quiet diplomacy to work "behind the scenes," and occasionally, they make public appeals on behalf of individuals or about specific themes or countries. From 1981 to 1997, Carter was directly responsible for the release of approximately *50,000* political prisoners whose human rights had been violated, according to Douglas Brinkley, author of *The Unfinished Presidency*.

- President Carter was a strong proponent of the establishment of the post of High Commissioner for Human Rights at the United Nations, and the Center has worked closely with the three High Commissioners since 1995. The Center has organized four expert consultations with and for the Office of the HCHR as part of its long-standing commitment to help strengthen international human rights systems. A larger conference on human rights defenders is planned for November 2003 in Atlanta.

- The Carter Center and President Carter have been strong advocates since 1996 for the International Criminal Court. The Center sent representatives to Rome in 1998 for the negotiations on the ICC statute and has collaborated with other international nongovernmental organizations to build global support for the court. President Carter has sent dozens of letters to heads of state, encouraging them to ratify the ICC statute. The court was formally established July 2002, and the first 18 judges were inaugurated in February 2003. President Carter wrote letters of congratulations and encouragement to each of the judges, as well as the first ICC prosecutor, Mr. Luis Moreno Ocampo.

- Mrs. Carter advocates for the abolition of the death penalty in the United States and on behalf of juveniles and mentally ill individuals on death row. She contacts state legislators in support of proposed laws to ban the juvenile death penalty and urges governors to commute the death sentences of juveniles and mentally ill individuals around the country. Given geographic and racial disparities in the imposition of capital punishment at the national level, President Carter also supports a moratorium on the federal death penalty.

- President Carter is a member of the Reebok Human Rights Award Board of Advisors. A Carter Center human rights attorney serves as his delegate to help select the Reebok Award recipients each year.

U.N. PRIZE IN THE FIELD OF HUMAN RIGHTS

For his lifelong commitment to human rights, President Carter was recognized by the United Nations as the 1998 recipient of the prestigious U.N. Prize in the Field of Human Rights. The prize is awarded every five to 10 years to individuals or organizations for their dedication and effectiveness in promoting and protecting human rights. Past recipients include Amnesty International and Nelson Mandela. The 1998 prize was particularly important because it fell on the 50th anniversary of the Universal Declaration of Human Rights.

THREE

FIGHTING DISEASE

Across the globe, President Carter and the Carter Center have improved quality of life through programs that work to eradicate and control infectious diseases, health education projects teaching people to prevent disease, and agricultural training to multiply crop yields. These activities build hope among the world's poorest people by alleviating unnecessary suffering and showing people how they can take steps to transform their own lives.

The Center leads a worldwide campaign that has achieved a 98 percent reduction of Guinea worm disease in Africa and Asia. Through the River Blindness Program, the Carter Center has assisted in the delivery of more than 40 million treatments of Mectizan® in Africa and Latin America. Applying experience and knowledge gained from Guinea worm eradication and river blindness control efforts, the Trachoma Control Program fights blinding trachoma in Africa and Yemen. The Carter Center tackles two additional diseases in Nigeria - lymphatic filariasis and schistosomiasis - and through the Ethiopia Public Health Initiative, the Center conducts public health training.   Farmers are learning improved agricultural techniques to grow more food for their families and boost the economy in sub-Saharan Africa, while in the Center's Mental Health Program seeks to improve the services and treatment for the millions of people and their families who suffer from mental illnesses every year.

GUINEA WORM ERADICATION PROGRAM

Guinea worm disease is set to become only the second disease to be wiped off the face of the earth. The "fiery serpent," as it is commonly called throughout the world, has been around for centuries. It's even been found in 3,000-year-old Egyptian mummies.   The numbers afflicted by this debilitating disease have been reduced worldwide by 98 percent, from 3.5 million cases in 1986 to less than 65,000 in 2001. Guinea worm will be the second disease to be eradicated from the world (after smallpox) and the first disease to be overcome without "magic-bullet" vaccines and medications.

The Carter Center began its on-the-ground fight against Guinea worm disease in Pakistan and Ghana in 1987. Today, the Center leads the effort worldwide. Much of the Center's work is concentrated in countries with the heaviest burden of disease: Sudan, Ghana, and Nigeria.

Guinea worm is a painful and debilitating disease whose effects reach beyond a single victim, crippling agricultural production and school attendance, for example. A child suffers and is unable to attend school. Or his parent suffers, unable to harvest crops or attend to younger children. The village suffers a food shortfall when its people are unable to work.

During one year in the mid-1980s in southeastern Nigeria, rice farmers lost $20 million (U.S.) due to outbreaks of Guinea worm disease.

Guinea worm disease is contracted when stagnant water, contaminated with microscopic fleas carrying infective larvae, is consumed. Inside a human's abdomen, the larvae mature and grow, some as long as three feet. After a year, the worm slowly emerges through an agonizingly painful blister in the skin.

Some worms can take up to two months to be completely expunged. The burning sensation caused by the emerging worm leads many victims to immerse their limbs in water, seeking relief, but the cycle of infection only begins again as the worm releases more larvae into the water.

Preventing Guinea worm disease seems simple: don't enter the water with an emerging Guinea worm and don't drink unfiltered water. But the challenge lays in educating villagers to always filter their water and ensuring they have the necessary filters to do so. Teaching these practices can come in conflict with traditional beliefs; for example, some villagers believe Guinea worm disease is the result of sorcery. Carter Center staff help train local health workers to use educational materials to explain the cause of Guinea worm disease and to treat those who are infected. They also treat stagnant ponds with monthly larvacide treatments.

The Carter Center helps to provide the essential ingredients for a successful eradication campaign—political will, financial support, and technical expertise. Its partners in the fight against Guinea worm disease help make this work possible. The government of Japan provides funding, water wells and vehicles, while the Japan Overseas Cooperation Volunteers provide hands-on support. Major assistance is also being provided by the U.S. Peace Corps volunteers. There are also numerous ongoing corporate and private donors. E.I. du Pont de Nemours & Company and Precision Fabrics Group have given filter cloth valued at more than $14 million; BASF has provided the larvacide Abate®, valued at more than $2 million; Johnson & Johnson has donated enough medical supplies-like Tylenol®, forceps and gauze-to treat more than 3,000 villages; Hydro Polymers has provided 9 million pipes to provide personal water filters; and the Gates Foundation has given generous funding.

RIVER BLINDNESS PROGRAM

The Carter Center is one of the few organizations fighting onchocerciasis, commonly known as river blindness, in both Africa and Latin America, working in all endemic areas in the Americas, which include Colombia, Ecuador, Guatemala, Mexico, Venezuela, and Brazil. Of the 18 million people infected with river blindness worldwide, 500,000 are blinded or visually impaired. The Carter Center is part of a global effort to eliminate the disease as a public health problem by 2007.

River blindness is spread through the bite of a small, black fly that breeds in rapidly flowing rivers and streams along the most fertile banks. When a fly bites, millions of microscopic worms are released into the body, causing incessant, debilitating itching. The worms can cause eyesight damage and potential blindness, when they enter the eyes. The economic and health consequences of this disease are devastating as adults cannot farm or care for their children. Fertile riverbanks are abandoned for fear of contracting the disease, and people move to less fertile grounds, disrupting a stable village economy.

Ivermectin, known by its trade name, Mectizan®—is the only known drug available to treat river blindness without severe side effects. Mectizan does not affect adult worms, but a single oral dose each year kills the microscopic infants, thus stopping the onset of blindness and the skin disease. The company that produces Mectizan®, Merck & Co., has generously donated the drug treatments to the world for as long as there is a need. Since the Carter Center began its River Blindness Program in 1996, the Center has enabled the delivery of more than 40 million treatments of Mectizan®—handling more treatments than any other organization combating this disease.

In June 2001, a panel of international experts that comprise the Carter Center's International Task Force for Disease Eradication, concluded that it is feasible to completely eradicate river blindness in the Americas if the treatment programs can treat at least 85 percent of the people living in endemic areas can be treated with Mectizan® twice a year.

The Center launched the Global 2000 River Blindness Program as part of a worldwide coalition, including the World Health Organization, the Lions Clubs International Foundation, and the World Bank. It maintains field offices in Guatemala, Cameroon, Nigeria, Sudan, Ethiopia, and Uganda to help local residents and health workers distribute Mectizan®. In Africa the program has worked extensively with the World Bank to secure funding for the African Program for Onchocerciasis control (APOC) to establish community-based programs and in Latin America it oversees a regional coalition known as the Onchocerciasis Elimination as the Onchocerciasis Elimination Program for the Americas (OEPA).

Trachoma is the world's leading cause of preventable blindness. The World Health Organization (WHO) estimates that 15 percent of all blindness in the world is caused by trachoma. Only cataracts cause more blindness worldwide but, unlike cataracts, trachoma can be prevented through improvements in personal and environmental hygiene. Trachoma is a bacterial infection which is easily spread from person to person. If a person suffers repeated infections over a period of years, scar tissue forms on the inside of their eyelids. The scar then contracts, causing the eyelashes to turn inward, often resulting in painful abrasion of the cornea and, in severe cases, untreatable blindness.

Today, almost all of the 146 million persons who suffer from trachoma live in developing countries in Africa, the Middle East and Asia. The public health and economic impact of trachoma is enormous, doing harm to entire communities. Less than 20 percent of farmers blinded from trachoma are able to farm. The Carter Center's Trachoma Control Program works with Ministries of Health and other partners in Ghana, Mali, Niger, Ethiopia, Sudan, and Nigeria to promote improvements in personal and environmental sanitation, and to deliver antibiotics to people at risk for blinding trachoma. The Trachoma Control Program also worked in Yemen from 2000-2003. The Carter Center's work in preventing blindness from trachoma is made possible through generous grants from Lions Clubs International and the Conrad N. Hilton Foundation.

LYMPHATIC FILARIASIS ELIMINATION PROGRAM

Lymphatic filariasis (elephantiasis) is a debilitating and deforming disease caused by infection from a parasitic worm. The infection is transmitted from person to person by mosquitoes. The parasite lives in the victim's lymphatic system. In its severest form, lymphatic filariasis causes elephantiasis—or dramatic swelling of limbs (usually the leg) and genitals (usually the scrotum). These conditions have a devastating effect on the quality of life of those affected, impacting them not only physically, but also emotionally and economically. The disease affects 120 million people in 73 endemic countries worldwide of Africa, Asia, the Western Pacific and Latin America. More than 41 million of those cases are in Africa. An additional 900 million people are at risk. Lymphatic filariasis is ranked by the World Health Organization (WHO) as the second-leading cause of permanent and long-term disability.

Fortunately, transmission of the infection can be halted by treating infected individuals once a year, for four to six years, with a single-dose combination of oral medicines. The drug combinations include diethylcarbamazine (DEC) and albendazole, DEC and ivermectin, or albendazole and ivermectin. The main drug for this infection is Mectizan® in combination with albendazole. Basic preventive measures, such as the use of bed nets and/or curtains (pre-impregnated with insecticide) also help control transmission of the infection. In patients with elephantiasis, binding affected limbs with compressive bandages and practicing proper hygiene helps reduce swelling and discomfort.

Lymphatic filariasis is one of the only six infectious diseases in the world considered eradicable. To help meet that goal, the Carter Center's Global 2000 Program is working to help eliminate lymphatic filariasis in Nigeria, the country with the greatest number of persons infected in Africa. Similar to its work to combat river blindness, Global 2000 is working with the government, health authorities, and villagers to establish and implement community-based drug treatment plans. Field staff will emphasize health education and the training and supervision of local village health workers.

The hope is that within 15 years lymphatic filariasis will no longer be a public health problem in Nigeria.

SCHISTOSOMIASIS CONTROL PROGRAM

Schistosomiasis is the second most devastating parasitic disease in tropical countries, after malaria. An estimated 200 million people in 74 tropical countries are infected: 100 million of these are in Africa. It is an excruciating and debilitating disease mostly affecting school-age children. The parasite penetrates the human skin exposed to contaminated water. It lives for years in the veins near the bladder or intestines, where it lays thousands of spiny eggs that tear and scar tissues of the intestines, liver, bladder, and lungs. Many victims suffer from poor growth and development, bladder dysfunction, and kidney disease.

Although schistosomiasis cannot be eradicated, it can be controlled and treated with a single annual dose of praziquantel. The Carter Center's Global 2000 program is working in Nigeria, since the need is greatest there. Global 2000 staff is testing children for blood in the urine using "dipsticks" and have has found that half of all Nigerian villages are infected. More than six million praziquantel tables are needed to treat those in just two states. In addition, Global 2000 is working with Nigerian health authorities on education programs to prevent the disease.

ETHIOPIAN PUBLIC HEALTH TRAINING INITIATIVE

The Carter Center's Ethiopia Public Health Training Initiative (EPHTI) emerged from discussions between former U.S. President Jimmy Carter and

Prime Minister Meles Zenawi, who subsequently invited the Carter Center to assist in the development of new programs to train health center staff for the entire country. Because less than half of Ethiopia's population has access to modern health services, the Government of Ethiopia (GOE) launched a major effort to expand primary health care services to under-served rural populations by establishing more than 500 new health centers. The expansiveness of the GOE project has made it difficult to recruit experienced training staff, particularly for the four colleges located in rural areas. With Its Ethiopian partners, the Carter Center began implementation of EPHTI with two major objectives in mind:

- Strengthening teaching capacities of the colleges' Ethiopian teaching staff; and
- Collaborating with Ethiopians in developing curriculum materials specifically created to meet the learning needs of health center team personnel.

The underlying principle of EPHTI's capacity-building strategy is that Ethiopians should play the primary role in meeting the country's community health needs. To this end, EPHTI seeks to create environments in which senior international experts work side-by-side with Ethiopian teaching staff to train health center teams in-country and develop learning materials based on Ethiopian experience and directly relevant to Ethiopia's health problems. In turn, the health center staff carry the responsibility of training and supervising all community health workers, including traditional birth attendants and community health agents. Thus, the basic training for health center teams given in the colleges has a direct and immediate impact on all modern primary health services throughout the country, even extending to villages and homes.

EPHTI objectives are accomplished through workshops, seminars, and conferences held on the various college campuses. In the workshops, Ethiopian teaching teams analyze the essential tasks necessary to manage each health problem and construct training modules that include the necessary knowledge, attitudes, and skills necessary for health teams to carry out their roles in typical settings in rural Ethiopia. EPHTI will assist the college teams in revising and testing draft materials at the campuses between periodic workshops, prior to final publication for use in the field.

The first workshop in 1997 focused on developing plans for the first four years of what is expected to be a ten to twelve year project. Seven workshops held at the Nazareth, Gondar, Dilla, Alemaya, and Jimma campuses over the past three years produced or began working drafts of training modules on topics such as:

- 30 core classroom training modules for multi-disciplinary teaching of health center team students on major diseases, proper health processes, and problems faced by rural health service centers and community-based health programs in Ethiopia;
- 30 sets of clinical and epidemiological case studies that complement the training modules;
- Several training manuals on essential health center functions for use in the field;
- 35 sets of standardized lecture notes for classroom teaching.

The Ethiopia Public Health Training Initiative is making significant contributions to capacity building in five higher education institutions. It is laying a solid foundation with participating individuals clearly expressing their "ownership" of the process and products.

AGRICULTURAL

The Sasakawa-Global 2000 Agricultural Program, also known as SG 2000, provides the tools and means to help farmers in sub-Saharan Africa increase their crop yields, sometimes two or even threefold. By increasing the amount of quality food produced, poverty will be lessened, food security enhanced, and national resources protected. SG 2000 works to:

- Provide/Promote the use of fertilizer, seed, and crop protection chemicals in food crops
- Restore soil fertility with increased use of fertilizer and with organic and indigenous mineral sources
- Advocate environmentally friendly agronomic methods of crop production, such as no-till
- Promote quality grain storage to sustain market prices for the farmer and ensure greater food security
- Promote the establishment of farmers' associations for marketing and saving and loan services, and
- Advocate the use of high quality food crops such as QPM maize that has greater protein quality than regular maize.

SG 2000 works with Ministries of Agriculture and national extension services to oversee country projects, rather than setting up a parallel organization outside the government, to ensure maximum benefit and minimum waste. SG 2000 and a government first draw up a memorandum of understanding that lays out the responsibilities of both parties. SG 2000 is working in Mali, Guinea, Ghana, Benin, Nigeria, Ethiopia, Uganda, Tanzania, Malawi, and Mozambique.

SG 2000's projects work in phases, beginning with establishing better crop production, training extension workers, then establishing production demonstration plots. They then increase their activities to include grain storage, crop processing, and seed production when appropriate.

CROP PRODUCTION DEMONSTRATIONS

SG 2000 teams up with farmers who agree to provide labor and land— 1,000 to 5,000 square meters—in order to try out new methods. Farmers can gain first-hand knowledge of different technologies and the associated costs, while reaping double, or even tripled, crop yield, by working in this way directly with extension workers. In each community, 30-40 farmers take part in the test plots. From 1986-2000, more than 500,000 demonstration plots had been established. SG 2000 promotes both conventional and no-till methods of crop production where each is appropriate. No-till employs the use of effective but short-lived herbicide to kill weeds, leaving a mulch on top of the soil, into which crops can be planted. This method:

- Increases soil moisture

12

- Reduces soil erosion
- Decreases soil compaction and improves soil tilth
- Reduces carbon dioxide release resulting in reduced greenhouse warming
- Conserves energy
- Reduces run-off resulting in less contamination of ground water, and
- Reduces production costs without reducing yields.

AFTER THE HARVEST

Increasing crop yield only solves part of the problem. A bumper harvest may be lost because of lack of proper on-farm storage. Without storage, crops must be quickly hauled from local markets to cities or other areas, but roads are poor, and vehicles are scarce and expensive. Through SG 2000, extension workers have learned how to construct inexpensive but durable one to two-ton storage bins that give protection against insects and rodents. Proper storage, along with improved handling of harvested grain and chemical treatment against insects can sharply reduce spoilage. Before these techniques were used 20 to 40 percent of the yield was lost.

FARMERS ASSOCIATION DEVELOPMENT

Encouraging farmers to organize into groups is an important aspect to SG 2000's work. Farmer groups have better bargaining power in negotiating seed and crop prices, and are better able to market their crops. Farmer associations in Benin have 35,000 members and have started their own savings and loan programs. Their deposits exceed $1 million, and members are required to make regular deposits. Only members are allowed to take out a loan, and strong social and kinship bonds ensure that loans are repaid. In Ghana, farmers belonging to an association are able to get loans from the national agricultural development bank, and association members are responsible for repayment as a group.

COLLABORATION

The SG 2000 programs cooperate with agrobusiness companies in the production of seed, and the supply of chemical inputs. In order to keep abreast of new information, and bring resource-poor farmers the best plant materials and technology, SG 2000 collaborates with other programs in different countries, and with international research organizations such as the International Research Centers. The Center works particularly closely with CIMMYT (The International Maize and Wheat Improvement Center) on the introduction of QPM materials to provide better quality protein to the consumers. QPM has protein equivalent in quality to that found in milk and is especially beneficial for child development.

MENTAL HEALTH PROGRAM

Back in 1971 when Rosalynn Carter began working on mental health care issues, few people even spoke the words "mental health." "Mental health" meant only mental illness, and mental illness was shrouded in such shame and stigma that many people neglected the issue. Today, much has changed. A family consumer movement started in the early 1980s; research has given us tremendous knowledge about the brain and new medications; and mental health services have improved significantly.

Yet, much remains to be done. People with mental illnesses still face great stigma and discrimination. The importance of mental health promotion is under recognized, and insurance providers often do not provide parity for mental health treatment. In the United States alone, mental illness is the second leading cause of disability, and mental disorders affect one in five Americans, according to the first-ever Surgeon General's report on mental health, released in December 1999.

Mrs. Carter continues her advocacy efforts through the Carter Center's Mental Health Program, founded in 1991. The program focuses on mental health policy issues with four strategic goals:

- To reduce stigma and discrimination against people with mental illnesses
- To achieve equity for mental health care comparable to other health care
- To advance promotion, prevention, and early intervention services for
- children and their families
- To increase public awareness worldwide about mental health and mental
- illness and to stimulate local actions to address those issues.

The Program pursues its goals on state, national, and international levels. The Rosalynn Carter Georgia Mental Health Forum, established in 1995, is held every May for state mental health organizations. The Forum has addressed such topics as "Children's Mental Health: Generating Hope through Shared Responsibility," "Improving Access for Georgians," and "Recovery: A Journey for Life."

Mrs. Carter's desire to coordinate the efforts of national mental health leaders and organizations led to her initiating the annual Rosalynn Carter Symposium on Mental Health Policy in 1985. The success of the Symposia led to the formation of Mental Health Program in 1991. The Symposia, held every November, have examined such issues as assuring quality in mental health care, mental health and illness in the workplace, privacy and confidentiality of patient information, and promoting healthy behaviors in children.

To guide the Symposia and other Mental Health Program activities, Mrs. Carter established the Mental Health Task Force in 1991. The Task Force, funded by the John D. and Catherine T. MacArthur Foundation, identifies major issues in the field, convenes meetings, and develops initiatives to reduce stigma and discrimination. Retired Task Force members who wish to remain active in the Mental Health Program's activities are invited to join the National Advisory Council.

In addition to the annual Symposia, the Mental Health Program also hosts public outreach programs as part of the Center's annual Conversation series. Topics have included "Coping with the Stigma of Mental Illness," featuring author Kathy Cronkite and actor Rod Steiger sharing their personal experiences with clinical depression and "Breaking Through the Stigma: Portrayal of Mental Illness in the Media."

At the international level, the Inaugural World Conference for the Promotion of Mental Health and Prevention of Mental and Behavioral Disorders was held at the Carter Center in December 2000. The second world conference was held September 11-13, 2002 in London. Also since its establishment in 1992, Mrs. Carter has chaired the International Women Leaders for Mental Health, a Committee of the World Federation for Mental Health Consisting of Royalty, Heads of State, and First Ladies.

In addition to working with mental health professionals, the Program awards eight fellowships every year, six to U.S. journalists and two to journalists from New Zealand who are writing or producing works on mental health issues. Reporters often are the best communicators to the general public, and the works resulting from The Rosalynn Carter Fellowships for Mental Health Journalism can greatly reduce stigma and better inform people about pressing issues.

FOUR

BUILDING HOPE

As President of the United States, Jimmy Carter was deeply committed to social justice and basic human rights. He and Mrs. Carter left the White House in search of meaningful ways to contribute in these areas. In addition to promoting peace and human rights through the Carter Center, they lead the Jimmy Carter Work Project (JCWP) for Habitat for Humanity International (HFHI) one week each year.

Carter's involvement with Habitat for Humanity International began in 1984 when the former president led a work group to New York City to help renovate a six-story building with 19 families in need of decent, affordable shelter. That experience planted the seed, and the Jimmy Carter Work Project has been an internationally recognized event of HFHI ever since. Each year, the Carters give a week of their time—along with their building skills—to build homes and raise awareness of the critical need for affordable housing. The JCWP is held at a different location each year, and attracts volunteers from around the world. Carter and volunteers built 92 houses in Anniston, Ala., LaGrange and Valdosta, Ga., during JCWP 2003 June 8-14. The 2002 JCWP took place in Africa. One thousand houses were built in 18 countries, with the final 100 houses constructed in a five-day build in Durban, South Africa. In 2001, JCWP built 136 houses at six sites across South Korea with more than 9,000 volunteers participating from around the world. Other recent JCWP builds have taken place in New York-Florida-Georgia (2000—157 houses), the Philippines (1999—293 houses) and Houston, Texas (1998—100 houses).

"We have become small players in an exciting global effort to alleviate the curse of homelessness," Carter has said. "With our many new friends, we have worked to raise funds, to publicize the good work of Habitat, to recruit other volunteers, to visit overseas projects and even build a few houses."

Since leaving office, Carter has gained a reputation as a tireless champion for social justice. "Habitat has successfully removed the stigma of charity by substituting it with a sense of partnership," Carter has noted. "The people who live in the homes work side-by-side with the volunteers, so they feel very much that they are on an equal level."

Habitat for Humanity International is a non-profit, ecumenical Christian housing ministry dedicated to eliminating substandard housing and making decent shelter a matter of conscience and action. Habitat has built more than 150,000 houses worldwide. Volunteers work with future homeowners to build or renovate houses, which are then sold to partner families at no profit, with no interest charged on the 15-20 year mortgage. The money from the sale of each house goes into a revolving Fund for Humanity, to support future building projects.

Carter once said, "Habitat has opened up unprecedented opportunities for me to cross the chasm that separates those of us who are free, safe, financially secure, well fed and housed, and influential enough to shape our own destiny from our neighbors who enjoy few, if any, of these advantages of life. I get a lot more recognition for building houses in partnership with people than I ever got for the Camp David Accord or for Salt II or for all our projects in Africa or Asia or anything I do now since I left the White House. I can walk down the aisles of airplanes talking with people and invariably the number one thing that everybody says is, 'Tell me about Habitat.'"

FIVE

PRESIDENT CARTER'S DOMESTIC POLICY ACHIEVEMENTS

When President Carter entered the Oval Office, the United States encountered a variety of domestic and international issues:

- there was no national energy policy, and America was becoming more and more dependent on foreign oil;
- little public trust existed in the honesty and openness of government
- Washington was slow in implementing vital programs and policies;
- severe social issues were being lacking attention or were inadequately addressed by the previous Republican administrations;

- the national defense had been weakened due to a defense budget which had been annually decreasing in real terms;
- the NATO Alliance was not as strong as it had been in years past;
- the differences between Israel and Egypt continued to pose a risk of war; and
- a firm United States response to human rights violations was not a priority.

Over his 4-year term, clear progress was seen in solving the following problems:

- nearly all of Carter's comprehensive energy program was passed by Congress, and the Department of Energy was created to oversee the program;
- belief in the government's integrity returned, and faith in the government's openness and fairness was restored
- the government became more productive and efficient: the Civil Service system was totally revised for the first time in the 20th century; 14 reorganization initiatives were proposed to the Congress, passed, and implemented; two new Cabinet departments were created to combine and modernize the government's response to energy and education issues; inspectors general were placed in all Cabinet departments to take on fraud, waste and a variety of other corrupt practices; the regulatory process was improved through the organization of the Regulatory Council, the carrying out of Executive Order

12044 and its necessity for cost-impact analyses, abolishment of unneeded regulation, and enactment of the Regulatory Flexibility Act; a series of steps were established to insure the public's participation in government; and the process of deregulating the airline, trucking, rail and communications industries was undertaken;

- crucial social issues, many continually ignored by Washington, were given immediate attention; an inner-city policy was conceived and instituted to stop the decline in our cities; the Social Security System received sufficient funding to give it a solid financial basis; the Humphrey-Hawkins Full Employment Act was passed; Federal assistance for education increased by over 75 percent; the minimum wage rose to levels required to relieve the results of inflation; affirmative action became a major priority.

- more African-Americans, Hispanics and women were named to senior government jobs and confirmed as judges than ever before in U.S. history; the deadline to pass the ERA was extended to help the ratification attempt; and minority business hired by the Federal government increased by over 100%;

- the country's first sectoral policies were installed, for the auto and steel industries, as Carter's Administration showed the benefit of cooperation among the government, business and labor;

- halting trends from previous Republican administrations, real defense spending went up every year throughout his term;

- the NATO Alliance displayed its unity in reacting to challenges in Eastern Europe and Southwest Asia and in approving the issues to be considered in the finalization of the Helsinki Final Act;

- the Camp David Accords and the Peace Treaty signed by Egypt and Israel was bolstered in two areas: continual advancement in the normalization of Egyptian-Israeli ties in several fields, and the word of both Egypt and Israel, in tandem with the help of the United States, to work towards a successful agreement regarding the autonomy talks for the West Bank and Gaza;

- the Panama Canal Treaties were passed, which significantly bettered relations with Latin America;

- Carter redoubled the United States' longtime promise to monitor human rights around the world, evenhandedly and objectively, leading many other countries to give their human rights policies a high priority;

- America's determination to oppose aggression, such as the Soviet Union's unwarranted invasion of Afghanistan, was illustrated by quick and severe responses.

During the 1970's the U.S. endured a successions of economic shocks never before seen in peacetime. The event having the greatest impact was the explosive rise of OPEC oil prices. Also, there were global commodity shortages, natural disasters, agricultural shortages and serious challenges to world peace and security. America's skill in handling these shocks was hampered due to a decline in the growth of productivity and the continuance of persistent inflationary forces that had been in place over the prior 15 years before Carter became president.

Still, the economy demonstrated itself to be considerably resilient. Real output increased at an average rate of 3 percent annually after Carter assumed office, and unemployment dropped by about 10 percent. The country saw the creation of about 8 million productive private sector jobs. The most difficult economic problem that Carter faced—inflation—can now be seen in better perspective after the passing of over 20 years since Carter's term ended.

In his book, *Jimmy Carter's Economy*, author W. Carl Biven notes the views of Herbert Stein, Richard Nixon's chief economic adviser. Stein has stated that despite inflation and the slowdown in productivity growth in Carter's final year in office, what many consider to be the best simple measure of the economy—real per capita income after tax—increased between 1976 and 1980. There is absolutely no question that the high interest rates that peaked in 1980 were in large part the result of OPEC enacting massive increases in the cost of oil, which could not have been prevented by any administration in office at the time.

EMPLOYMENT

During his four years in office Carter dedicated himself to address the needs of workers and provide further job opportunities to those in need of work. From January, 1977, until January, 1981:

- over 8 million new jobs were created.
- total employment rose to 97 million. Women, minorities and young adults made the most gains. Employment over that four-year period rose by:
  - 17% for adult women
  - 11% for blacks, and
  - 30% for Hispanics
  - black teenagers saw an employment rise of more than 5%, halting the slide that took place from 1969 to 1977

Major initiatives begun by Carter were largely responsible for these accomplishments and provided a strong platform for employment and training policy in the 1980's. In Carter's first year in office, 1977, as a component of the comprehensive economic stimulus program:

- there were 425,000 public service jobs made available
- 200,000 jobs were supported by a $1 billion youth employment initiative
- Job Corps positions increased 100%, and 1 million summer youth jobs were funded—a 25 percent increase.

In 1978:

- the Humphrey-Hawkins Full Employment Act was passed
- the $400 million Private Sector Initiatives Program started

- a targeted jobs tax credit for impoverished youth and others with special employment needs was enacted
- the Comprehensive Employment and Training Act was renewed for four years.

In 1979:

- a $6 billion welfare reform proposal began with financial support for 400,000 public service jobs
- welfare reform demonstration projects began in cities around the nation
- Vice President Mondale started a nationwide study of youth unemployment in the U.S.

In 1980:

- the Vice President's Task Force learned firsthand the major education and employment hardships that exist for underprivileged and minority youngsters. To assist them, a $2 billion youth education and jobs initiative was created to give unemployed youth with the education and work experience necessary for them to land good jobs in the 1980's.
- As a component of the economic revitalization program certain steps were enacted to assist workers in high unemployment areas:
- an extra 13 weeks of unemployment benefits for those who were unemployed for a longer period than expected.

- $600 million to train the underprivileged and unemployed for newly-created private sector jobs.
- positive adjustment demonstrations to assist workers in slumping industries.
- The important Title VII Private Sector Initiatives Program was renewed for an another two years.

Along with making considerable progress in aiding the disadvantaged and unemployed, notable improvements were seen by all workers:

- an unprecedented national agreement with organized labor enabled the opinions of working men and women to be voiced as the country's economic and domestic policies were created.
- the Mine Safety and Health Act ensured better working conditions for the country's half million miners.
- significant reforms of the Occupational Safety and Health Administration were achieved to help lower unnecessary burdens on companies and to concentrate on major health and safety issues.
- the minimum wage rose from $2.30 to $3.35 an hour from 1977 to 1981.
- the Black Lung Benefit Reform Act was passed.
- attempts to cripple the Davis-Bacon Act were stopped.

TRADE

In 1980, U.S. trade made gains as a result of solid export upswings in manufactured and agricultural goods. Agricultural exports attained a new mark of over $40 billion, and manufactured exports increased by 24 percent to a new high of $144 billion. In these categories the United States realized strong surpluses of $24 billion and $19 billion respectively. While U.S. oil imports were a strain on the country's foreign exchange receipts, that depletion was somewhat offset by a 19 percent reduction in the volume of oil imports.

U.S. trade negotiators obtained good results in 1980 in guaranteeing effective fulfillment of the deals agreed to during the Tokyo Round of Multilateral Trade Negotiations. Agreements entered into with Japan, for example, ensured that the United States was able to increase its exports to the Japanese market in important divisions such as telecommunications equipment, tobacco, and lumber. The success of U.S. trade negotiators also convinced several developing countries to approve several of the non-tariff codes agreed to during the Multilateral Trade Negotiations. This guaranteed that these countries would increasingly take on obligations in regard to the international trading system.

A difficult global economic environment created an obstacle for the management of trade relations. U.S. trade negotiators overcame serious problems in the area of steel, and helped ensure that U.S. chemical exports had ongoing access to the European market.

Constant briefings with the private sector in our country allowed U.S. trade negotiators to zero in on potential roadblocks to U.S. trade in services, and to install a foundation for future negotiations. Services became an increasingly vital source of export receipts for the United States, and the Carter Administration continually fought for more access to foreign markets.

SMALL BUSINESS

Carter often remarked, "There is nothing small about small business in America." These companies created nearly 50% the country's gross national product; over 50% of new technology; and well over 50% of the jobs created by industry.

Since this area of the economy was and is so crucial, Carter pursued policies that evened the playing field for smaller firms. These specific efforts were a pivotal part of his program to reenergize the economy.

They included his campaign to reduce considerably the time consuming bureaucratic paperwork imposed on business. They consisted of his mandate to ambitiously increase the governmental contracting dollars directed to small firms, in particular those operated by women and minorities. And they included his proposals to revitalize existing small businesses and to aid the development of new ones as a result of tax reform; financing assistance; market expansion; and the backing of product innovation.

Many of Carter's initiatives to spur the development and growth of small businesses resulted from the White House Conference on Small Business, which he convened. Carter started the implementation of a majority of the ideas generated by that citizens advisory body.

MINORITY BUSINESS

One of Carter's most satisfying achievements was his Administration's policies that sparked the growth and fortifying of minority business. His was the first Administration to rank this issue as a high priority in policy agenda. To implement the gains of the early agreements in this field he submitted legislation to Congress aimed at further creation of minority business.

His administration reorganized the Office of Minority Business into the Minority Business Development Administration in the Department of Commerce. MBDA proved to be a key player in helping minority businesses attain equitable competitive footholds in the marketplace.

Washington's procurement from minority-owned companies nearly tripled during Carter's term. Federal deposits in minority-owned banks grew by over 50% and minority ownership of radio and television stations increased by nearly 50%. The SBA-run 8(a) Pilot Program for procurement with the Army was very successful and he eventually increased the total sum of agencies involved to include NASA and the Departments of Energy and Transportation.

Carter firmly believed then and now that the most direct way to full freedom and equality for our country's minorities resides with the opportunity of minority communities to take part competitively in the free enterprise system. He was and is a firm advocate of the idea that Washington has a fundamental responsibility to help in the building of minority business.

CREATING ENERGY SECURITY

The foremost legislative priorities of the Carter Administration centered on sweeping changes in U.S. energy activities and the unprecedented formation of a national energy policy. Under Carter, the U.S. finally faced the issue of its over reliance on foreign oil. He led the country to pursue different types of energy production—coal, crude oil, natural gas, solar, nuclear, synthetics—with energy conservation a major focus.

NATIONAL ENERGY POLICY

Carter's work with Congress resulted in the country's first national energy policy:

- Under his program of phased decontrol, on September 30, 1981, domestic crude oil price controls came to an end. As a consequence, exploratory drilling activities attained an record high;

- Costs for new natural gas were decontrolled as a result of the Natural Gas Policy Act—and natural gas production reached what was then an all time high; the supply deficits of the 1970's were eliminated;

- The windfall profits tax on crude oil was passed, providing $227 billion over the 1980's for aid to low-income households, more mass transit support, and a mammoth investment in the production and creation of alternative energy sources;

- The Synthetic Fuels Corporation was founded to assist private companies in erecting facilities to manufacture energy from synthetic fuels;
- Solar energy funding increased fourfold, solar energy tax credits were became law, and a Solar Energy and Energy Conservation Bank was formed;
- A route was selected to deliver natural gas from the North Slope of Alaska to the U.S. mainland;
- Coal production and consumption incentives were increased, and coal production reached the highest point in history;
- A gasoline rationing plan was passed by Congress for potential use in case of a massive energy supply shortage or interruption;
- Gasohol production was hugely increased, with the goal turning it into 10 percent of all unleaded gasoline;
- New energy conservation incentives were given to citizens, businesses and communities, with the result being that conservation rose dramatically. The U.S. reduced oil imports by one quarter—or 2 million barrels daily—during Carter's term.

INCREASED FORMATION OF DOMESTIC ENERGY SOURCES

Carter insisted that the U.S. lower its reliance on imported fossil fuels while switching to domestic renewable sources of energy, but also directed the change to be made in an orderly, economic, and environmentally sound way. This led the Administration to launch a number of initiatives.

Leasing of oil and natural gas on government property, especially the outer continental shelf, was sped up while the Administration revised leasing procedures as a result of the amendments made in 1978 to the Outer Continental Shelf Lands Act. The following year, the Interior Department conducted six OCS lease sales, the highest number ever, which brought in federal receipts of $6.5 billion, another all-time high. The five-year OCS Leasing timetable was set up, requiring 36 sales over a five-year period.

Carter ordered the total restructuring of the government's coal leasing program to lead it into compliance with the statutes of the 1976 Federal Land Planning and Management Act and other mandatory provisions. The program was created to equalize the competing interests that impact resource development on public property and to ensure that a large enough supply of coal would be on hand to fulfill national needs. This led in 1981 to the first competitive government coal lease sale since the early 1970's.

Carter's efforts led to the Energy Security Act of 1980, which formed the Synthetic Fuels Corporation. The Corporation was charged with sparking the creation of commercial technologies for manufacturing of synthetic fuels, among these being liquid and gaseous fuels that emanate from coal and the making of oil from oil shale. The Act infused the Corporation with a first payment of $22 billion to attain these goals. The Energy Security Act also gave substantial incentives for the creation of gasohol and biomass fuels, which increased the country's supply of alternative energy sources.

COMMITMENT TO A SUSTAINABLE ENERGY FUTURE

Carter's 1977 National Energy Plan represented an historic change from the policies of previous presidents. The plan underscored the importance of both energy production and conservation to reaching the foremost national goal of depending primarily on domestic sources of energy. The National Energy Plan led to energy conservation becoming the hallmark of Carter's national energy policy.

In 1978 he began a Solar Domestic Policy Review. This marked the first advancement towards a national launch of renewable energy sources into the U.S. economy. The Review resulted in the 1979 Solar Message to Congress, the first of its type in U.S. history. The Message described the Administration's solar program and set an ambitious goal of receiving one-fifth of our country's energy from solar and renewable sources by the 21st century. The mission of the federal solar program is to assist industry in creating renewable energy sources by stressing basic research and development of solar technologies, one being photovoltaics, which create energy directly from the sun. Simultaneously, as a result of tax incentives, teaching the public about its importance, and the Solar Energy and Energy Conservation Bank, the solar program was designed to lead state and local governments, business, and individuals to increase their employment of solar and renewable resource technologies.

Due to the effectiveness of these policies and procedures, the energy efficiency of the U.S. economy increased significantly and investments in renewable energy sources rose notably. By 1981, it required 3 1/2 percent less energy to create a constant dollar of GNP than it did four years earlier. This rise in efficiency provided a savings of more than 1.3 million barrels per day of oil equivalent, approximately the level of all oil production that took place in Alaska in 1981. During Carter's term, government support for conservation and solar energy rose by more than 3000 percent, to $3.3 billion by 1981, which encompassed tax credits for solar energy and energy conservation financing.

COMMITMENT TO NUCLEAR SAFETY AND SECURITY

Major advancements under Carter's direction were reached in addressing three crucial problems that came about from the employment of nuclear energy: radioactive waste coordination, nuclear safety and weapons proliferation.

In 1977, Carter outlined his nuclear nonproliferation policy and began the International Fuel Cycle Evaluation. In 1978, Congress enacted the historic Nuclear Nonproliferation Act.

In 1980, Carter sent his nuclear waste management program to the Congress. This program was a considerable improvement over all previous efforts. The primary components of that policy were: acknowledging the severity of the problem and the variety of technical and inherent issues; creating a technically and environmentally conservative plan to the first permanent repository; and giving the states with major involvement in nuclear waste disposal issues a forum by forming the State Planning Council.

In response to the accident at Three Mile Island, Carter created the Kemeny Commission to study the accident and provide recommendations. Almost all of the Commission's substantive proposals were approved by the Administration and were undertaken by the Nuclear Regulatory

Commission. The Congress passed the President's proposal for the Nuclear Regulatory Commission, and the Nuclear Safety Oversight Committee was formed to determine that the Administration's policies were put into place.

While envisioning a vast increase in international demand for U.S. steam coal, Carter learned that congestion must be eliminated at primary U.S. coal exporting ports. His Administration commissioned the Interagency Coal Task Force Study to increase cooperation and management of resources among shippers, railroads, vessel broker/ operators and port operators, and to decide the most suitable government role in enlarging and modernizing coal export companies, with special attention given to dredging deeper channels at certain ports. The Task Force's success enabled the Corps of Engineers to lower considerably the amount of time needed for studying port dredging proposals. The Administration also proposed that the Congress pass legislation to grant the President generic authority to suggest funding for channel dredging operations.

ENHANCING BASIC HUMAN AND SOCIAL NEEDS

Carter believed that before his Administration, many of America's basic individual and social needs were ignored or managed insensitively by Washington. Over his four years in office, he substantially increased funding for a large number of vital programs; created new programs where existing ones had proved to be insufficient; aimed Federal dollars to those citizens and regions most in need of financial assistance; and eliminated barriers that for no reason kept an unacceptable number of disadvantaged citizens from receiving support for their most fundamental needs.

The Carter Administration brought upon clear advancements in the attempt to solve some of America's most prevalent human and social problems. By working with Congress, Carter showed that Washington could meet the basic human and social needs of individuals in a prompt and compassionate way.

NATIONAL HEALTH PLAN

While in office Carter pursued a goal of Harry Truman's by proposing to Congress a National Health Plan, one that would have allowed the U.S. to attain the goal of comprehensive, universal health care coverage. The legislation Carter offered created the basis for such a comprehensive plan and directed attention towards the most crucial problems of health financing and delivery. It did not promise too much or spend too much. His National Health Plan consisted of the following important features:

- nearly 15 million extra disadvantaged citizens would have obtained fully-subsidized comprehensive coverage;
- pre-natal and delivery services were provided for all pregnant women and coverage is given for acute care for babies in their first year of life;
- the elderly and disabled would have a ceiling placed on yearly out-of-pocket medical costs and would no longer encounter limits on hospital coverage;
- all full-time workers and their families would be given insurance for major medical expenses under required employer coverage;

- Medicare and Medicaid would be merged into one program, Healthcare, for improved program efficiency, accountability and uniformity;

and

- significant cost controls and health system revisions would be installed, including better incentives for Health Maintenance Organizations.

Carter requested Congress to compare his Plan with the others— programs which either accomplished not enough to better the health care requirements of Americans most in need or programs which would inflict too great a financial load on U.S. taxpayers.

HEALTH CARE COST CONTROL

Throughout Carter's Administration, legislation he submitted to lower health care cost inflation remained one of his top priorities, but was turned down by Congress. Taking the longer view, Carter claimed that the health care reimbursement organization had to be reformed. He called for a departure from inflationary cost-based reimbursement and payment-for-service, toward a plan of future reimbursement, under which health care providers would work within preset budgets. Reimbursement reform, according to Carter, was vital to ultimately restraining inflation in the price of health care.

HEALTH PROMOTION AND DISEASE PREVENTION

During Carter's term, the Surgeon General issued "Healthy People," an historic report on health promotion and disease prevention. The study highlighted the growing general agreement that America's health strategy needed to be revised to stress the importance of the prevention of disease. Specifically, the study proposed a 10-year plan of reasonable goals aimed at lowering the mortality rate.

Carter asked Congress to support the guidelines of "Healthy People," and to implement the recommendations to reach its goals. He reiterated that this would require adoption of a broader view of health care, to incorporate such issues as environmental health, workplace health and safety, commercial product safety, traffic safety, and health education, promotion and information.

MATERNAL AND CHILD HEALTH

When Carter entered the White House, immunization levels for preventable childhood diseases had dropped to 70%. Due to a focused national program during his Administration, at least 90% of children 15 years and younger, and almost all school-age children were immunized. Also, reported cases of measles and mumps dropped to the lowest levels on record.

Under the National Health Plan Carter proposed, there would not have been any cost-sharing for prenatal and delivery services for all expectant mothers and for acute care given to babies in their first year of life. These preventive services were known to have tremendous success in terms of bettering newborn and long-term child health.

Carter sent to Congress the Child Health Assurance Program (CHAP), which was approved by the House. In this program, an extra two million underprivileged children under 18 would have become eligible for Medicaid benefits, and additional special health assessments. CHAP would have in addition improved the uninterrupted care of nearly 14 million children who were then eligible for Medicaid. An extra 100,000 poor pregnant women would have gained eligibility for prenatal care with this program.

Carter fully supported two extremely successful programs: special supplemental food services for women, infants and children (WIC) and Family Planning. The food benefits under WIC proved beyond doubt that it effectively prevented poor health and therefore lowered ensuing medical costs. The Family Planning program showed itself to be effective at lowering unwanted pregnancies among poor women and teenagers.

EXPANSION OF SERVICES TO THE POOR AND UNDERSERVED

During Carter's Administration, health care for the poor and underserved rose considerably. The number of National Health Service Corps (NHSC) workers providing services in medically underserved regions multiplied from 500 to nearly 3,000 over four years. The number of citizens assisted by the NHSC increased more than three times from 1977 to 1981. There was a 100% rise in the number of Community Health Centers offering services in especially underserved regions, reaching approximately six million people by the end of his term.

MENTAL HEALTH

One of Carter's crowning health achievements was the passage of the Mental Health Systems Act, which evolved out of proposals presented by his Commission on Mental Health. Rosalynn Carter's championing of this legislation directly contributed to its enactment.

The Act was created to start a new relationship between Washington and the states in the devising and implementing of mental health services. Also, the Act specifically offers assistance for prevention and support programs to the chronically mentally ill to stop unneeded institutionalization and for the development of civic-based mental health services.

HEALTH PROTECTION

With Carter's complete support, Congress passed "Medigap" legislation, which calls for voluntary certification of health insurance policies supplemental to Medicare, to restrain widespread abuses in this field.

Carter's leadership in the area of toxic agent control led to the passage of a bill with potential cost-saving significance. This bill created a "super-fund" to cover hazardous waste cleanup costs.

In the category of accidental injury control, Carter created automobile safety standards and provided funding to increase enforcement of a national speed limit. Studies estimated that these policies saved over 13,000 lives and prevented over 100,000 serious injuries annually.

FOOD AND NUTRITION

Carter's leadership led to a bill calling for the widespread reform of the Food Stamp Program, which Congress enacted in 1977. Not content with that, Carter teamed with Congress in 1979 and 1980 to pass many other important alterations to the Program. These changes reduced considerable red tape, lowered the rates of fraud and error, enabled the program to be more sensitive to the needs of senior citizens and disabled, and increased the ceiling on permissible program expenditures.

DRUG ABUSE PREVENTION

At the start of Carter's Administration there were more than 500,000 heroin addicts in the United States. By making a concerted effort to decrease the supply of heroin, in addition to offering treatment and rehabilitation to addicts, the number of heroin addict went down noticeably, with a drop in heroin overdose deaths by 80%, and a decline in heroin related injuries by 50%.

EDUCATION

Carter's leadership was evidenced in his partnering with the Congress to pass landmark education legislation. His Administration underscored the necessity of education by forming a new Department of Education. The Department gave education a larger presence in Washington, while ensuring the actual control and oversight of education to states, localities, and private schools. The Department successfully merged nearly 150 Federal education programs into an orderly, streamlined operation that is more able to handle the needs of teachers and students. The Department stressed its goal of reducing red tape and paperwork and in turn to accelerate Federal funding to school districts and institutions of higher learning.

Carter's prodding resulted in the passage of two major bills—one supporting elementary and secondary education and the second, postsecondary education. The Education Amendments of 1978 represented almost all of his Administration's efforts for improvements in the Elementary and Secondary Education Act, including specific new programs to aid students' achievement in the basic skills and to assist school districts with particularly high levels of children from poor families. The Middle Income Student Assistance Act, increased eligibility for need-based Basic Educational Opportunity Grants to nearly one-third of the students participating in post-secondary schooling and enabled many more students to finally become eligible for a variety of grants, work-study and loans.

Carter's leadership is reflected in his working with Congress for more than two years on a major reauthorization bill that provides extra benefits to postsecondary education. The Education Amendments of 1980 includes Carter's recommendations for enhancing the Higher Education Act—such as proposals for easier loan access for students; an inaugural parent loan program; streamlined application processes for student financial aid; an invigorated Federal commitment to emerging colleges, especially the historically black institutions; a new approval for equipment and building modernization funding for the country's top research universities; and improved international education programs.

Augmenting these legislative achievements were important administrative directives designed to decrease paperwork and simplifying policies aligned with Federal education programs. He also began major initiatives to lower the amount of defaulted student loans, and to also reduce fraud, abuse, and waste in education programs.

With considerable foresight, Carter, to see that education would be prepared to face scientific and technological advancements in the future, ordered a major review of the status of science and engineering education nationwide. His goal was to ensure that the discoveries from this report would function as a springboard for necessary reforms at every level of education.

Carter's leadership resulted in the attainment of the financial means required to meet many of his legislative and administrative goals. Carter requested the greatest overall increase in government funding for education in U.S. history. His budget items were especially sensitive to the requirements of certain populations such as minorities, women, the educationally challenged and those from lower income families, those with disabilities, and students who for whom English is a second language. Also, he requested meaningful increases for several programs created to improve the quality of American education, including programs dealing with important subjects as varied as international education, research libraries, museums and teacher centers.

In 1980, Carter proposed to Congress an innovative legislative initiative that would steer $2 billion into education and job training projects created to reduce youth unemployment through better connections between schools and the work place. Although this proposal received bipartisan support, it was not voted on in the final, hectic days of the 96th Congress. Carter reiterated that only by building a basic skills education program in tandem with work training and employment incentives could America see substantial headway made in ending one of the most critical social afflictions in our country—youth unemployment, especially among minorities. Much progress was seen after the passage of the Youth Employment and Demonstration Project Act of 1977 and the ensuing rise in Federal investment in youth employment programs.

SOCIAL SECURITY

One of the top priorities for Carter was to maintain the effectiveness and efficiency popularly associated with the social security program, and to guarantee current and future beneficiaries that the program will still be vibrant when their time comes to receive benefits. Carter led a strong effort to improve the benefits of many social security recipients during his term as president.

Shortly after becoming president, Carter proposed and Congress passed legislation to guard the solvency of the old age and survivors trust fund and stop the imminent depletion of the disability insurance trust fund, and to fix a flaw in the benefit formula that could harm the long-term health of the social security system as a whole. The program submitted by Carter played a major role in stabilizing the system. That legislation was eventually enhanced by the Disability Insurance Amendments of 1980, which reinforced the disability insurance program even more, and decreased certain disparities among beneficiaries.

Carter always opposed reductions in basic social security benefits and taxing social security benefits. He maintained support for the yearly indexing of social security benefits.

Carter proposed major tax changes to increase the means of financing for business investment. While understanding the need for fiscal restraint, his budget took the initiative for creating a long-term tax reduction program aimed to build capital formation.

Therefore, he proposed an historic amount of generous tax allowances for depreciation, as well as simplified depreciation accounting, raising the allowable rates by roughly 40 percent. Carter also called for revision of the investment tax credit, allowing it to be refundable, to satisfy the investment needs of companies without any current earnings. He believed these two proposals, in addition to phased-in tax reductions for individuals, would aid economic efficiency and tax equity.

WELFARE REFORM

In 1979 Carter proposed a welfare reform package that offered help to many of the severe problems in the welfare system. This proposal was presented in two bills, The Work and Training Opportunities Act and The Social Welfare Reform Amendments Act. The House enacted the second proposal, but not the first. Within the structure welfare system at the time, Carter's reform proposals presented achievable ways to increase self-sufficiency with work as opposed to welfare, gave more assistance to those unable to work, resulted in the removal of inequities in coverage under programs of that time, and provided fiscal relief required by states and localities.

Carter admitted the welfare system that he inherited was long overdue for complete reform. The legislation he proposed could very well have helped end inequities by creating a national minimum benefit, and by directly connecting benefit amounts to the poverty threshold. It was designed to lower program complexity, which results in inefficiency and waste, by easing and coordinating administration between different programs.

CHILD WELFARE

Carter's leadership led to vastly improved child welfare services and foster care programs and to the forming of a Federal system of adoption assistance. Congress passed H.R. 3434, the Adoption Assistance and Child Welfare Act of 1980, demonstrating that the plight of children in need of homes and their permanent placement was a top concern of his Administration. This bill helped greatly reduce the possibility that children would not be lost in the foster care system, but rather reunited with their families whenever possible or placed in new and loving adoptive homes.

LOW-INCOME ENERGY ASSISTANCE

In 1979 Carter proposed a bill that would give yearly sum of $1.6 billion to poor families which are most impacted by skyrocketing energy costs. With the help of Congress, heating bill assistance was immediately provided to eligible households in time before the start of winter.

Reacting to the summer heat wave of 1980, one of the worst on record, Carter ordered the Community Services Administration to provide over $27 million to help low income individuals, especially senior citizens, facing life threatening situations because of extreme heat.

HOUSING

Despite the high interest rates that afflicted the economy during Carter's years in office, his final record shows that with his teaming with Congress, the regulatory agencies, and the financial community, his Administration achieved an increased and more constant stream of funds into home mortgages. Deregulation of the interest rates payable by banks, the evolution of variable and renegotiated rate mortgages, development of high yielding savings certificates, and growth of the secondary mortgage market all improved housing's ability to attract funding and guaranteed that mortgage money would not stopped when interest rates went up. Those actions decreased the wide swings of the housing market. Further, Carter obtained legislation modernizing Washington's emergency authority to give support for the housing industry by way of the Brooke-Cranston program, and initiating a new Section 235 housing stimulus program. These programs allowed Washington to respond quickly and efficiently with serious setbacks in vital industry.

Carter also stressed the need to provide homeownership opportunities for all citizens. By employing innovative financing tools, such as the graduated payment mortgage, increased access to housing credit was provided to middle-income families. By replenishing the Section 235 program, almost 100,000 middle-income households had the ability to buy new homes. By reducing paperwork and red tape in Federal programs, and by teaming with State and local governments to relax the regulatory burden, Carter deserves credit for keeping down housing costs and making available affordable housing during the turbulent economic climate—sparked by international developments—of the 1970s.

As a large result of Carter's leadership, 5.5 million more American families purchased homes between January of 1977 and January of 1981 than in any equivalent time span in history. Also, over 7 million homes started construction during his Administration, 1 million more than were built over the prior four years.

Carter went to extreme lengths to meet the housing needs of poor and middle-income families. During Carter's term, over 1 million subsidized units were made available for rent by poor Americans and over 600,000 assisted units went into construction. In addition, his Administration implemented a series of policies to revitalize and maintain the country's 2 million units of public and assisted housing.

TRANSPORTATION

Carter's leadership led Congress to approve of the Airline Deregulation Act of 1978, the Motor Carrier Act of 1980, and the Harley O. Staggers Rail Act of 1980, beginning a new era of reduced regulation of transportation industries. Deregulation resulted in increased productivity and operating efficiencies in these industries, and stimulated price and service competition, with consumers profiting immensely.

MASS TRANSIT

The country's public transit systems' ridership rose at an annual average of 1.1% each year in the 1970's (6.9% in 1979). Carter foresaw that continued increases in the cost of fuel would make transit an expanding part of the nation's transportation system.

To meet that scenario, Carter projected a ten-year, $43 billion program to raise mass transit capacity by 50 percent, and to steer industry towards more energy efficient vehicle uses in the 1980's. The first segment of this proposal was the five-year, $24.7 billion Urban Mass Transportation Administration reauthorization legislation Carter sent to Congress in March, 1980.

Carter's Administration was also the first to have seen enacted a non-urban formula grant program to help rural areas and small communities with public transportation programs to stop their reliance on the automobile, promote energy conservation and efficiency, and offer transportation services to poor rural communities.

Carter noted the growing need in rural and small towns for improved transportation services. Rail freight service to many areas declined as railroads abandoned unproductive branch lines. Simultaneously, rural roads were often seen to be inadequate to accommodate large, heavily-loaded trucks. The increased need for "harvest to harbor" service also placed more of a burden on rural transportation systems, while bottlenecks along the Mississippi River slowed down grain shipments to the Gulf of Mexico.

Carter improved the situation with the following steps:

- He requested that the Department of Transportation's new Small Community and Rural Transportation Policy target federal aid for passenger transportation, roads and highways, truck service, and railroad freight service to rural areas. This program implemented and built upon the earlier White House Initiative, "Improving Transportation in Rural America," undertaken in June, 1979, and Carter's "Small Community and

Rural Development Policy," which was approved in December, 1979.

- To further develop the nation's waterways, Carter authorized the building of a new 1,200 foot lock at the site of Lock and Dam 26 on the Mississippi River. When opened in 1987, the new lock provided a capacity of 86 million tons annually, an 18 percent increase over the former system. The U.S. Army Corps of Engineers also began studies to determine the feasibility of enlarging the Bonneville Locks. Rehabilitation of John Day Lock was finalized in 1982.

MARITIME POLICY

During his term Carter sought to make certain that the U.S. maritime industry would not have to operate at an unfair competitive disadvantage in the world market. As he indicated in his maritime policy statement to Congress in July, 1979, the American merchant marine is vital to our nation's welfare, and actions by Washington should assist rather than hurt it. To meet this goal, Carter signed into law the Controlled Carrier Act of 1978, allowing the Federal Maritime Commission to regulate certain rate cutting practices of some state-controlled carriers, and in 1980 signed a bilateral maritime agreement with the People's Republic of China that broadened the access of American ships to 20 targeted Chinese ports, and set aside for American flag ships a large share (at least one-third) of the cargo between our nations. This agreement led to an expansion of U.S. and Chinese shipping services linking the two countries, and generated further momentum to the increase of Chinese-American trade.

As a former Naval officer, Carter also saw the need to modernize and grow the dry bulk segment of the U.S. fleet. He noted that America's extreme dependence on foreign transport of U.S.-bulk cargoes prevented the U.S. economy from adding seafaring and shipbuilding jobs, increased the balance-of-payments deficit, deprived Washington of major tax revenues, and left the nation dependent on foreign-flag shipping for a constant supply of raw materials to aid the civil economy and war production in time of war.

COAL EXPORT POLICY

Carter formed the Interagency Coal Task Force Study to improve cooperation and management of resources among shippers, railroads, vessel broker/operators and port operators, and to decide the most beneficial Federal role in enlarging and modernizing coal export sites, including dredging deeper channels at certain ports.

WOMEN

Carter's leadership resulted in four years of swift advancement for women. His focus was two tiered: to provide women of the U.S. with an entire range of opportunities and to include them in the mainstream of every area of American life and leadership.

He appointed a record number of women to judgeships and to senior government positions. Twenty-two 22 percent of all his appointees were women, and he nominated 41 of the 46 women who served on the Federal bench beginning in his Administration. Never before had women held policymaking positions at the highest branch of every Federal agency and department.

Carter strengthened the rights of women working outside the home by consolidating and ordering enforcement of sex discrimination laws under the EEOC, by adding more employment rights of expectant mothers through the Pregnancy Disability Bill, and by increasing federal job opportunities for women by way of civil service reform, in addition to flex-time and part-time employment.

By executive order, Carter created the first nationwide program to offer women who run their own businesses technical assistance, grants, loans and better access to Federal contracts.

Carter paid particular attention to the needs of women who worked in the home. He initiated an Office of Families within HHS and called for a White House Conference on Families. He created a program targeting CETA benefits to assist displaced homemakers. The Social Security system was altered to end the widow's penalty and a comprehensive report on discriminatory provisions and possible corrections was sent to Congress. Laws were enacted giving divorced spouses of foreign service officials the ability to share in pension benefits.

Carter oversaw the establishment of an department on domestic violence within HHS to work with the 12 agencies that at that time had domestic violence relief programs, and also provided information on the problem and the range of assistance available to victims.

Carter consistently promoted the Women's Educational Equity Act and family planning activities, along with other programs that pertain to women, such as food stamps and social security.

Carter not only called for increased opportunities for American women, but also pursued a policy of equality for women internationally. On women's issues, he sought the advice of men and women in government and in the private sector from all parts of the U.S. He created two panels—the President's Advisory Committee for Women and the Interdepartmental Task Force on Women—to counsel him on those issues.

Though falling short in the end, no president fought harder for the passage of the Equal Rights Amendment than Carter. And when Carter called for national health care plan and a welfare reform program, he specifically insisted that these entities reflect the needs of women, especially advocating programs to help the victims of domestic abuse.

DISABLED AMERICANS

Carter's Administration, more than any previous one, led the charge toward full civil rights for disabled Americans in the workplace, and in all public facilities, so that disabled citizens could enter the American mainstream and contribute to the fullest their resources and talents to our economic and social life.

Just as he promoted, in unprecedented fashion, the civil rights of the disabled in schools and on the job, Carter sponsored other advancements in health prevention, such as his Administration's immunization and nutrition programs for young children, and also sought considerably more funding for research into the effort to reverse spinal cord injury.

FAMILIES

In 1980 Carter assembled the first White House Conference on Families, which consisted of seven national hearings, over 500 state and local events, three White House Conferences, and the direct involvement of over 125,000 citizens. His Administration also created the Office of Families within the Department of Health and Human Services to study government policies and programs that impact families.

OLDER AMERICANS

Carter's Administration made considerable headway in confronting the serious problems encountered by senior citizens. Early in his term he successfully worked with Congress to ensure sufficient revenues for the Social Security Trust Funds. And in 1980 strength of the Social Security System was bolstered by legislation he proposed to allow borrowing between the separate trust funds. He also signed into law legislation stopping employers from mandating retirement before age 70, and eliminating mandatory retirement for most government employees. In addition, Carter's efforts led Congress to amend the Older Americans Act in a manner that noticeably improved the management of its housing, social services, food delivery, and employment programs. Carter's budgets consistently called for increased funding for nutrition, senior centers and home health care.

REFUGEES

Carter's Administration undertook and implemented the first comprehensive reform of U.S. refugee and immigration policies in over a quarter century. He also formed the first refugee coordination office in the Department of State under the direction of a special ambassador and manager for refugee affairs and programs. These actions brought common sense and streamlining of America's previously disjointed, inconsistent and outmoded refugee and immigration policies.

With the unforeseeable arrival of thousands of Cubans and Haitians who came to American shores in 1980, not within the regular U.S. immigration and refugee admissions process, Carter's Administration displayed compassion in its response to an undeniable human emergency. Because of the steps taken to reorganize American refugee programs, the influx of immigrants was efficiently coordinated. He publicly thanked Americans for responding to this event with their trademark good will and hospitality, in addition to commending the private resettlement agencies who Carter regarded as indispensable in times of crisis.

Carter stated his belief that by and large immigrants to the U.S. contribute more toward making America stronger than they ever receive in benefits. He acknowledged that while the U.S. maintained a conviction to help immigrants whenever possible, simultaneously American immigration and refugee policies needed to be adhered to, with the support of sufficient enforcement resources. As a result of their enforcement policy, the illegal flow from Cuba was stopped and steps were taken to determine that U.S. refugee and immigration laws had been honored.

VETERANS

Carter understood the debt owed to the men and women who served America in the armed forces and sought to keep or restore peace in the world. His commitment to veterans, as seen by his record, is illustrated by a conscientious and steady emphasis in three general areas:

First, his Administration made certain to honor the Vietnam veteran. Under the direction of VA Administrator Max Cleland, Carter was proud to lead the U.S. in an overdue recognition America's gratitude to the soldiers who served the U.S. in Vietnam. But with the notice of their service went an understanding that a considerable number of Vietnam veterans have specific needs and problems. Carter's Administration was able to initiate a long pursued psychological readjustment and outreach program, widely respected for its popularity, sensitivity and success. The Administration also championed the cause of veterans who fought in Southeast Asia and were exposed to Agent Orange. Under Carter's direction, inquiries began that responded to veterans' questions regarding their health and provided the foundation for creating an effective compensation policy in a sensitive, expeditious and compassionate manner.

Second, his efforts led to the tailoring of the VA health care system to the requirements of the service-connected disabled veteran. Carter launched and saw put into place the first reform of the VA vocational rehabilitation system since its debut in 1943. Also, his Administration became the first to call for a cost-of-living increase for the beneficiaries of VA compensation every year. His Administration also formed the Disabled Veterans Outreach Program in the Department of Labor which compiled a strong record in finding employment for disabled veterans.

Third, the VA health care system, the most expansive in the free world, kept its independence and peerless performance during Carter's term. He ordered that the system become more efficient so as to be able to treat more veterans than ever before by focusing on out-patient care and by way of up-to-date operational improvements. He insisted that as the median age of American veterans continues to rise, that further alterations within the VA system would be necessary to keep it strong and to continue as a model to America and to the world as an entity for research, treatment and rehabilitation.

GENERAL AID TO STATE AND LOCAL GOVERNMENTS

Carter advocated a strengthening of the fiscal and economic condition of America's state and local governments. He met this goal by supporting economic development of local communities, and by calling for General Revenue Sharing and other vital grant-in-aid programs.

GRANTS-IN-AID TO STATES AND LOCALITIES

During Carter's Administration, total grants-in-aid to State and local governments rose by over 40 percent. This healthy increase in support permitted States and localities to keep services that are essential to the public without imposing overbearing tax burdens. It also let his Administration create an unprecedented partnership amongst the leaders of the Federal government and State and local government elected representatives.

GENERAL REVENUE SHARING

Carter's leadership led to Congress passing legislation that extended the General Revenue Sharing program. This program was the foundation of his efforts to support the fiscal health of America's local government. It allocated $4.6 billion annually to cities, counties and towns, and was indispensable to the continued ability of local governments to offer necessary police, fire and sanitation services.

URBAN POLICY

In 1978 Carter proposed the country's initial comprehensive urban policy. That policy consisted of over 100 improvements in existing government programs, four new Executive Orders and nineteen pieces of city-oriented legislation. Largely due to Carter's prodding, sixteen of those bills were passed.

ECONOMIC DEVELOPMENT

One of the major goals of Carter's domestic policy was to invigorate the private sector economic base of America's impoverished urban and rural regions. Because of Carter's efforts, there was an increase in the number of the Federal government's economic development programs which gave new tax incentives for private investment in urban and rural areas. These programs assisted many cities and towns in drawing new private sector jobs and investments and to keep jobs and investments that were in place.

When Carter took office in 1977, Washington spending less than $300 million a year on economic development programs, with only $60 million of those funds being directed to America's urban areas. By 1981, Carter established the Urban Development Action Grant (UDAG) program and considerably expanded the economic development programs in the Commerce Department.

COMMUNITY DEVELOPMENT

The teaming between Federal, State and local governments to bolster America's communities was a high priority of the Carter Administration. Carter's efforts led to the expansion of the Community Development Block Grant (CDBG) program and the passing of a $400 million Urban Development Action Grant (UDAG) program. Both of these programs supplied vital community and economic development aid to poor cities and counties through the U.S.

NEIGHBORHOODS

During Carter's Administration, a number of positive steps were taken to reach a full merging of neighborhood organizations and government at all levels. Carter successfully fought against housing discrimination. He launched an innovative Self Help funding program and technical resource transfer mechanisms. He established unprecedented methods of access for neighborhood organizations to attain a voice in Federal and State government decision-making. Neighborhood based organizations are the threshold of the American community.

RURAL POLICY

Beginning in 1977, Carter ordered an improvement in the effectiveness with which Washington responds to the problems and requirements of a speedily changing rural America. The fast growth of some rural regions caused a severe strain on communities and their resources. There were also continuing problems of poverty and economic stagnation in other regions of rural America.

In December, 1979, Carter announced the Small Community and Rural Development Policy. It was the culmination of several years' work and was designed to address the varying needs of our rural population. In 1980, his Administration worked with the Congress to pass the Rural Development Policy Act of 1980, which allowed government to meet the needs of rural people and their communities more effectively and efficiently.

As a result Carter's leadership, the following actions took place:

- Began the position of Under Secretary of Agriculture for Small Community and Rural Development to supply overall leadership.
- Established a White House Working Group to help in the enforcing of the policy.
- Partnered with more than 40 governors to create State rural development councils to team with the White House Working Group, and the Federal agencies, to more effectively deliver State and Federal programs to rural regions.

- Ordered the White House Working Group to once a year review existing and proposed policies, programs, and budget levels to decide their adequacy in meeting rural needs and completing the policy's objectives and principles.

This effort on Carter's part resulted in a first-of-its-kind policy. Rural affairs finally received the prominence it always needed. With the assistance and dedication of numerous people around the U.S. who were dedicated to rural affairs, Carter built a mechanism for effectively taking on rural problems.

CONSUMERS

In 1979, Carter signed an Executive Order intended to strengthen and coordinate Federal consumer programs and to install steps to improve and facilitate consumer participation in Administration decision-making. Forty Federal agencies started programs to meet with the requirements of the Order. These programs effectively dealt with consumer problems, gave more information to consumers, heightened opportunities for citizen participation in Federal proceedings, and ensured that the consumer perspective was addressed.

SCIENCE AND TECHNOLOGY

Carter recognized that Washington plays a special role in science and technology. His Administration ended a decade-long decline in funding, with real support of basic research increasing nearly 11% during his term in office. Also, Carter pushed to increase the funding of long-term research in the many mission agencies, with the goal of harnessing the American capacity for innovation to meet the economic, energy, health, and security issues that confront the U.S.

Under Carter, science and technology evolved into increasingly vital components of U.S. national security and foreign policies. This became more important in the age of sophisticated defense systems and of increasing dependence among all nations on modern technology for all phases of their economic strength. On these grounds, scientific and technological considerations became key elements of his Administration's decision-making in important national security and foreign policy issues such as the modernization of American strategic weaponry, arms control, technology transfer, the improving bilateral relationship with China, and American relations with the developing world.

Four themes helped mold U.S. policy in international scientific and technological cooperation: pursuit of new international programs to advance American research and development objectives; creation and strengthening of scientific exchange to overcome politically ideological, and cultural divisions between the U.S. and other nations; establishment of programs and institutional relations to assist developing countries in employing science and technology beneficially; and cooperation with other countries to oversee technologies with local impact. At Carter's direction, his Science and Technology Adviser constantly pursued international programs in advocating these four themes. Under Carter, the U.S. gave special effort to scientific and technical relations with China, to new means of scientific and technical teamwork with Japan, to partnering with Mexico, and other Latin

American and Caribbean countries, and to the Institute for Scientific and Technological Cooperation.

Carter believed that U.S. cooperation with developing nations reflected the emphasis that all of them placed on the linkage between economic growth and scientific and technological capability. It also upheld the view that the great strength of the U.S. in science and technology made better relations with the U.S. technical community a particularly productive way of improving this capability. Carter stressed that scientific and technological assistance are key common points of interest between the U.S. and the developing world, a connection that was not recognized prior to his Administration.

SPACE POLICY

Carter's Administration created a framework for a strong and improving space program for the future:

- The Administration's space policy confirmed the separation of military space systems and a civil space program, and simultaneously, gave new direction on technology information sharing among the civil and military programs. Carter's civil space program was based on three basic doctrines: first, space policy would reflect a coordinated strategy of applications, science, and technology development. Second, activities would be pursued when they could be uniquely or more efficiently conducted in space. Third, a premature commitment to a high risk, space-engineering endeavors along the costs of previous

Apollo missions was inappropriate. A new flexibility under Carter provided the means to consider new space applications, space science and other space exploration activities.

- Technology Development. Carter backed the technology development effort behind the first Shuttle. He emphasized that it presented one of the most sophisticated technological projects ever undertaken, and as a result, would eventually face technical problems. Carter continually secured the needed funds for the Shuttle throughout his Administration.

- Space Applications. Beginning in 1972, the U.S. conducted experimental civil remote sensing through Landsat satellites, and saw many successful applications. Recognizing this accomplishment, Carter ordered the installing of an operational civil land satellite remote sensing system, with the coordinating management role being held by Commerce's National Oceanic and Atmospheric Administration.

- Space Science Exploration. Carter achieved the following goals in space science: (1) he continued a challenging program of planetary exploration to enable us to learn the origin and evolution of the solar system; (2) he ordered the use of the space telescope and free-flying satellites to begin a new era of astronomy; (3) he saw the development of a better understanding of the sun and its relationship with the terrestrial environment; and (4) he ensured the Shuttle and Spacelab conducted basic research that enhanced earth-based life science investigations.

DISTRICT OF COLUMBIA

Carter worked to improve the relationship between the Federal government and the government of the District of Columbia so as to pursue the goals and spirit of home rule, and as a result, the District had more say regarding its own destiny than ever before. Carter attempted to convince enough states to ratify the Constitutional Amendment bestowing full voting representation in Congress to Washington residents, without success.

THE ARTS

Federal support for the arts was improved under Carter by expanding Federal funding and services to arts institutions, individual artists, scholars, and teachers by way of the National Endowment for the Arts. He successfully requested a broadening of its scope that would enable it to reach to a more diverse population. Also, Carter revived the Federal Council on the Arts and Humanities.

Carter's achievements in the arts include:

- Increased support of institutions that educate the public in the development and understanding of the arts;
- Encouraged the corporate community to participate in a comprehensive effort to attain truly diverse financial support for the arts;
- An exploration of a wide range of mechanisms to support the creative talent of Americans and create audiences for their exhibits;

- Strong, active backing of the National Endowments for the Arts;
- An offering of greater recognition and aid for the rich cultural tradition of the nation's minorities;
- Provided grants for the arts in impoverished neighborhoods.

THE HUMANITIES

Carter's support for the humanities validated his view of their essential place in American life.

In the allocation of funding, he gave particular emphasis to:

- Humanities education in schools, in reply to the great needs that grew in this area;
- Scholarly research formulated to better our understanding of the cultures, traditions, and historical forces at play in other countries and in the U.S.;
- Attracting attention to the physical disintegration of various aspects of American cultural heritage—books, manuscripts, periodicals, and other documents—and to the creation of techniques to stop the destruction and to preserve those items; and
- The distribution of educational programming in the humanities to growing American audiences through the employment of radio and television.

Carter requested that in making its grants, the Endowment would increase its emphasis on techniques that promote support for the humanities from non-Federal sources, in order to re-emphasize American tradition of private philanthropy in this area, and to guarantee and expand the financial capability of our cultural institutions and life.

INSULAR AREAS

Carter was and has continually been firmly in favor of self-determination for Puerto Rico, the Virgin Islands, Guam, American Samoa and the Northern Mariana Islands, and unfailingly supported the political aspirations that are democratically selected by their peoples. This principle was the foundation of the comprehensive territorial policy that Carter sent to Congress in 1980; the vast majority of the legislative components of that policy were agreed to by the 96th Congress.

REMOVING GOVERNMENT WASTE AND INEFFICIENCY

One of Carter's major priorities was to restore public faith in Washington by greatly reducing waste and inefficiency. Dramatic advances were made toward this goal during Carter's term, many of which had always been considered impossible to attain. In the areas in which government rules and operations were not needed, they were eliminated, as took place in the airline, rail, and trucking industries, and in financial deregulation. Where government functions were required, they were streamlined, through such landmark achievements such as the Civil Service Reform Act of 1978.

CIVIL SERVICE REFORM

In 1978, Carter proposed his Civil Service Reform Act to Congress, referring to it as the centerpiece of his attempt to reform and reorganize the government. The bill passed, and was implemented well ahead of the statutory schedule. Throughout the service, Carter maintained the necessity to ensure that reward and retention are based on performance and not simply on tenure on the job. In the first true test of the Reform Act, 98 percent of the eligible senior-level managers signed up for the Senior Executive Service, deciding to forego job protections for the motivation and possible reward for this new group of top executives. Some Federal agencies created merit pay systems for GS-13-15 managers, and most agencies instituted new performance goals for each of their employees. All agencies gave performance bonuses earned by the most accomplished members of the Senior Executive Service. Dismissals rose by 10 percent, and dismissals specifically for poor job performance went up 1,500 percent, after the Act was adopted. Finally, Carter proposed and saw implemented a fully independent Merit Systems Protection Board and Special Counsel to guard the rights of whistle-blowers and other Federal employees who encountered threats to their rights.

REGULATORY REFORM

Great strides were made in regulatory reform due to Carter's leadership. He ordered the elimination of former economic regulations that stifled competition and raised consumer costs, and he mandated strong management principles for the regulatory programs needed in the U.S. by reducing paperwork and other wasteful tasks.

Carter's economic deregulation program had major accomplishments in five areas:

Airlines: The Airline Deregulation Act stimulated healthy competition, saving billions in fares, and forcing the airlines to become more efficient.

Trucking: The trucking deregulation bill created competition in the industry and allowed truckers more freedom of choice on the routes they drive and the goods they haul. The bill also drummed out most of the former law's immunity for setting rates. The Congressional Budget Office estimated Carter's reforms saved at least $8 billion per year in 1981 dollars and lowered the inflation rate by half a percent.

Railroads: Before Carter became president, overregulation suppressed railroad management initiative, service, and competitive pricing. Carter's bill gave the railroads the freedom they desired to rebuild a strong, vibrant railroad industry.

Financial Institutions: Carter's leadership was largely responsible for passing two major types of financial reform legislation, legislation which laid the groundwork for the most sweeping changes in the financial services industry in over 40 years. The International Banking Act of 1978 was intended to lessen the advantages that foreign banks doing business in the United States had compared to American banks. The Depository

Institutions Deregulation and Monetary Control Act, adopted in 1980, provided for the step-by-step elimination of a number of anti-competitive obstacles to financial institutions and freedom to provide services to and bring in the business of consumers, particularly small savers.

Telecommunications: While Congress failed to pass legislation in this area, pressure by Carter was a key factor in the Federal Communications Commission taking bold action to open all components of communications to competition and to end regulations in the places where competition made them obsolete. The country benefited from a tremendous increase in competition and new services.

The other aspect of Carter's reform program pertained to the regulations that are required to guard the health, safety, and welfare of U.S. citizens. For these regulations, Carter's Administration developed a management program to reduce costs without sacrificing goals. Under his Executive Order 12044, agencies were ordered to analyze the costs of their primary new rules and consider other approaches, such as performance standards and voluntary codes, that in the end made rules less costly and more flexible. Carter also formed the Regulatory Analysis Review Group in the White House to examine the most expensive new rules and found ways to better them. The Regulatory Council was created to provide the first Federal listing of forthcoming rules and end overlapping and conflicting regulations. Agencies began "sunset" programs to eliminate antiquated regulations. Carter's actions encouraged public involvement in regulatory policy-making, and his reforms saved billions of dollars in regulatory costs and wiped out thousands of unnecessary regulations.

PAPERWORK REDUCTION

During Carter's Administration paperwork was reduced by 15 percent, and procedures were put in place to maintain this progress. The Paperwork Reduction Act centralized, in OMB, supervision of all agencies' information needs and improved OMB's authority to end needless forms. The "paperwork budget" process, which Carter created by executive order, employed the discipline of the budget process to the seemingly endless hourly billing imposed on the public, compelling agencies to scrutinize all paperwork every year.

TIGHTENING STANDARDS FOR
GOVERNMENTAL EFFICIENCY AND INTEGRITY

To develop a framework to implement energy policy, Carter consolidated an array of energy programs and proposed the forming of the Synthetic Fuels Corporation; to give education the emphasis it deserves and to simultaneously reduce HHS to less cumbersome size, Carter made education a Cabinet post; to make a better system for reducing waste and fraud, he reorganized audit and investigative duties by placing an Inspector General in each major agency. During Carter's term, 14 reorganization initiatives were proposed and all were passed by Congress. His Administration saved hundreds of millions of dollars by putting into effect businesslike cash management principles and imposed strict standards for personal financial disclosure and conflict of interest issues by top Federal officials.

PROTECTING BASIC RIGHTS AND LIBERTIES

Carter took great pride in the advances that were made in assuring equality and guarding the basic freedoms of all citizens.

* The Equal Employment Opportunity Commission (EEOC) and the Office of Federal Contract Compliance (OFCCP) were reorganized and reinforced and a permanent civil rights group was established in OMB.

* To prevent fragmented, erratic and duplicative enforcement of civil rights laws, three agencies had coordinative and goal-setting responsibilities in discrete areas: EEOC for all job-related activities, HUD for all those dealing with housing, and the Department of Justice for any other areas.

* With the passing of the Right to Financial Privacy Act and a bill limiting police search of newsrooms, Carter begun to set a sound, comprehensive, privacy program.

MARTIN LUTHER KING, JR.

Carter was the first president to call for a national holiday honoring Dr. Martin Luther King, Jr., acknowledging the role King played in leading America towards providing every citizen with civil rights and equal opportunities. Carter stated that King's commitment to human rights, peace and non-violence stood as a monument to his humanity and courage, and that as one of America's greatest leaders, believed it to be appropriate that King's birthday be celebrated as a national holiday. Two years after Carter left office, Congress moved on his proposal and passed the King holiday bill.

PRIVACY

Carter insisted that as U.S. public and private institutions collect mounds of information with the advancement of communications and computer technologies, that action needed top be taken to safeguard the personal privacy of our citizens.

During his term, the Carter Administration acted on Privacy Commission study and set a national privacy policy. Carter worked with Congress to pass legislation restricting wiretaps and police access to bank records and to reporters' files. Under Carter's watch, there was a massive cut in the amount of personal files held by the government and limited the transfer of personal information between Federal agencies. Carter also pushed the Organization for Economic Cooperation and Development to set international policy to protect the privacy of personal information that is sent across borders.

PROTECTING AND DEVELOPING OUR NATURAL RESOURCES

From the start of his Administration, Carter urged Congress to enhance and protect, as well as develop America's natural resources. In terms of the environment, Carter took special pains to balance the need for resource development with keeping a clean environment, and he spearheaded several actions to encourage this goal. Regarding agriculture, Carter took the steps required to help raise farm incomes and to raise U.S. agricultural production to record levels. Preserving the quality of our environment was among the most important goals of Carter's administration and of Congress. As a result of that effort, Carter had several historic milestones:

PROTECTION OF ALASKA LANDS

Carter's signature achievement related to the environment was the passage of the Alaska National Interest Lands Conservation Act, one of the most important conservation actions of the 20th century. At issue was the fate of millions of acres of pristine land, cherished wildlife populations, native cultures, and the hope that generations of Americans yet to be born would be able to enjoy the breadth and beauty of one of nature's wonders, the landscape of Alaska. As direct a result of Carter's leadership, Congress enacted the Alaska Lands Bill in 1980.

The Act protected 97 million acres of new parks and refuges, more than doubling the landmass of our National Park and National Wildlife Refuge Systems. The bill increased by three times the size of our national wilderness system, adding 56 million acres. And by including 25 free-flowing river sections to the Wild and Scenic River System, the bill nearly doubled the river mileage in that category. The Alaska Lands Act confirmed Carter's commitment to the environment and provided a compromise between protecting regions of unsurpassed beauty and permitting development of Alaska's oil, gas, mineral, and timber resources.

PROTECTION OF NATURAL RESOURCES

Along with the Alaska Lands Act, Carter also scored more successes by greatly expanding the national wilderness and parks systems. In 1978, Carter's leadership led Congress to pass the unprecedented Omnibus Parks Act, which made a dozen additions to the National Park System. The Act also produced the first two national trails since the National Trails System Act was passed a decade earlier. Also, in 1980, as a result of his Environmental Message from the previous year, the Federal land management agencies set aside nearly 300 new National Recreational Trails, and Congress established about 4.5 million acres of wilderness in the lower 48 states. Carter throughout his term emphasized the need for Federal support only when it was predetermined that water resource projects were economically and environmentally sound. Because Carter avoided unsound projects of this type, by 1979 his Administration had the means to propose the first new project starts in 4 years.

Carter's 1978 Water Policy Reform Message was well received by Congress. This Message set a new national water resources policy with these goals:

* to give top emphasis to water conservation;
* to weigh environmental needs and values more fully and in addition to economic factors in the designing and overseeing of water projects and programs;
* to boost cooperation between state agencies and Washington in water resources planning and management.

In addition to the Executive Office of the President setting 11 policy making criteria to review the recommended federal water projects, the Water Resources Council outlined and implemented a new set of Principles and Standards for water projects which each federal construction agency must adhere to, and improved regulations were formed to implement the National Historic Preservation Act and the Fish and Wildlife Coordination Act. That meant water resource projects had to be determined to be financially sound before an authorization or appropriation was proposed by his Administration.

ADDRESSING GLOBAL RESOURCE AND ENVIRONMENTAL PROBLEMS

The Global 2000 Report, undertaken in response to Carter's Environment Message, was the initial one of its kind. Never before had the U.S., or any other government, formed such a comprehensive, long-range study of the connected world issues of resources, population, and environment.

The Report's findings were extremely revealing. They foretold the giant leap in population and human needs that would be seen by the start of the 21st century, while also forecasting at the same time a receding in the earth's ability to satisfy those needs, unless a vast majority of nations of the world moved boldly to halt the trends that had developed through the 1970s.

The United States contributed actively during Carter's term to a series of U.N. conferences on the environment, population, and resources. Following his 1977 Environmental Message, the Administration development assistance programs added emphasis to natural resource management and environmental protection. His 1979 Environmental Message called attention to the alarming loss of world forests, particularly in the tropics. An interagency task force on tropical forests led to the forming of a U.S. federal program to promote conservation and wise oversight of tropical forests. Carter considered the U.S. to be a world leader in wildlife conservation and in the evaluation of environmental effects of government policies. Carter's 1979 Executive Order instructing U.S. government agencies to determine the effects of their major actions outside U.S. borders was another example of his leadership.

COMMITMENT TO CONTROL OF POLLUTION AND HAZARDOUS CHEMICALS

Carter made substantial progress towards cleaner air and water, after demonstrating to Congress the Administration's firm commitment to these important national goals. In addition, Carter personally called for the implementation of many new pollution compliance strategies such as alternative and innovative waste water treatment programs, the "bubble" concept, the "offset" policy, and permit consolidation, all of which were established to lower regulatory costs on the private sector.

One of the Carter's most pressing environmental challenges proved to be unsuitable hazardous waste disposal, to which the president ordered three responses. First, he proposed the Oil Hazardous Substances and Hazardous Waste Response, Liability and Compensation Act (the Superfund bill) to give total authority and $1.6 billion in funds to clean up deserted hazardous waste disposal areas. In 1980 Congress passed a Superfund bill, which Carter signed into law.

Second, Carter formed a hazardous waste policing strike force to make sure that when available, responsible companies are ordered to clean up sites that were potentially dangerous to public health and to the environment.

Third, subtitle C of the Resource Conservation and Recovery Act was enforced. The regulations of this act called for comprehensive controls for hazardous waste and, in tandem with strict compliance, with a goal of preventing any future Love Canal scenarios.

THE REPORT CARD

Carter maintained that the people of the 1970's were entrusted with the protection of an irreplaceable environment and natural heritage. He stated unequivocally that ensuing generations were dependent upon a commitment from that era, the late stages of the 20th century, to protect and enhance the quality of our environment. Carter hoped that when his Administration was reviewed in the new millennium, that with hindsight it was evident:

*   that he built on America's pledge to the restoration of environmental quality;
*   that he protected the public health from the ongoing dangers of toxic chemicals, from pollution, from hazardous and radioactive waste, and that his policies helped make American communities safer, healthier and more desirable places to live;
*   that he protected America's wilderness areas and especially the last great frontier, Alaska, for the benefit of future generations;

* that he blazed the path for America to a sustainable energy future, one based more and more on renewable resources and on energy conservation;

* that he moved to preserve America's countryside and shoreline from poor management and wanton destruction;

* that he altered the management of Americas water resources toward water conservation, sound development and environmental preservation; and

* that he took forceful action in regard to global problems such as the ruination of forests, acid rain, carbon dioxide build-up and nuclear proliferation.

POLICY INITIATIVES

Many major agricultural policy reforms were initiated by Carter, with a goal of helping farmers lessen the impact of inflation in production costs. They provided an unmistakable strengthening of America's food and agricultural policy. These initiatives consisted of:

* Food Security Reserve: Carter proposed and Congress authorized the compiling of a 4 million ton food grain reserve for utilization in foreign food assistance. This reserve enabled the United States to maintain its food assistance commitment to nations lacking in food, even during times of short supplies and inflated prices. This corrected a major flaw in past U.S. food assistance policy.

* Comprehensive Crop Insurance: In 1980 Carter also proposed and Congress approved an important new crop insurance program. This

117

measure gave farmers a new type of support for helping them shoulder the financial risks that are inherent in agriculture. It replaced a variety of disaster programs that entailed all-too-many shortcomings.

* Special Loan Rates: Another bill that Carter proposed in 1980 was passed by Congress, which empowered the Secretary of Agriculture to offer higher loan rates to farmers who placed their grain in the farmer-operated grain reserve. This extra incentive to participate considerably helped strengthen the reserve.

* Increased Loan Prices: In 1980, Carter directed the increase of loan prices for wheat, feedgrains, and soybeans to help lessen the effects of a severe cost-price squeeze. Simultaneously, the release and call prices for the grain reserve were regulated upward.

IN REVIEW

The food and agricultural actions proposed by Carter left a solid foundation for future governmental movements in this area. The farmer-owned grain reserve demonstrated itself to be an especially effective way of stabilizing grain markets.

SIX

PRESIDENT CARTER'S FOREIGN POLICY ACHIEVEMENTS

Carter's policies were directed at three areas of specific change:

* the steady growth and continued movements abroad of the Soviet military, one which grew faster than America's over the previous two decades.

* the overwhelming reliance of Western countries, which by then increasingly included the United States, on crucial oil supplies in the Middle East.

* the pressures of change in several countries of the developing world, in Iran and doubt about the future stability of many developing nations.

As a result of those undeniable facts, Carter encountered some of the most severe challenges outside of war in the history of the United States. The Soviet invasion of Afghanistan posed a strong threat to East-West relations, and to regional stable flow of oil. An overwhelming vote in the U.N. General Assembly demonstrated that nations across the world, especially the nonaligned, considered the Soviet invasion as a threat to their sovereignty and security. Upheaval within the region next to the Persian Gulf posed risks (as it does in the 21st century) for the security and economic well being of all oil-importing countries and in turn for the entire global economy.

For Carter, the essence of America was its determination to move on, and knowing that prosperity, progress and most important of all peace could not be obtained by standing still. He constantly affirmed that a world of various countries struggling to preserve their independence, and of peoples seeking economic progress and political freedom, was not a world opposed to the principles and interests of the United States.

There were many positive developments during Carter's term in foreign affairs:

* U.S. alliances with the world's most advanced and democratic nations from Western Europe to Japan grew stronger than ever.
* Carter forged dramatic improvement in the relationship between Egypt and Israel and an historic framework towards a comprehensive Arab-Israeli settlement.
* The U.S. formally recognized China, building on the initiative undertaken by President Nixon.

* Across southern Africa, Carter worked for the peaceful change to majority rule in a context of regard for minority as well as majority rights.

* Carter took action domestically as well as with our allies to tackle the energy crisis by conservation and diversification of energy provisions based on internationally agreed targets.

* Carter demonstrated the U.S. commitment to protect Western interests in Southwest Asia, and notably increased American ability to do so.

* Although his last year in office was marred by the taking of U.S. hostages in Iran, Carter nonetheless could eventually claim that all were released unharmed, without the U.S. having to resort to any type of arms-for-hostages schemes that were seen in the Reagan Administration.

* Carter's leadership resulted in an energy program which was comprehensive and far-reaching. New institutions were formed such as the Synthetic Fuels Corporation and Solar Bank. Price decontrol for oil and gas was accomplished. American consumers met the challenge, resulting in real progress in consumption patterns.

* Followed up the plan first proposed in the Nixon Administration of returning control of the Panama Canal to its rightful owners through the Panama Canal Treaties.

* Unlike any president before or since, Carter championed the cause of human rights protection around the world.

THE U.S.-SOVIET RELATIONSHIP

In his book, "From the Shadows," Robert Gates, who served on the White House staff under four presidents and was Director of the CIA under the first President Bush, said he feels that historians and the general public have not appreciated Carter's contribution to the fall of the Soviet Union and the winning of the Cold War. Gates noted that Carter became the first U.S. chief executive to publicly and continually challenge the legitimacy of the Soviet leadership. His human rights policy, following up on the important and widely unrecognized position established by the Helsinki Final Act, by the statements of numerous Soviet and East European dissidents and individuals who became democratic leaders in the ensuing years, challenged the moral authority of the U.S.S.R. and gave U.S. sanction and assistance to those who protested against their totalitarian government. Whether a Soviet dissident of no stature or a widely known Soviet scientist, Carter's actions inspired them to press on. The effectiveness of the policy is best determined by the shrill response of the Soviet government, which understood better than Western leaders, the threat to them of this bold U.S. policy.

This wasn't just idle talk from Carter. He backed up his statements taking on the Soviet leadership with tangible support. Overtly, he provided the funding needed for American-sponsored radio stations to transmit directly into the U.S.S.R. and Eastern Europe. Covertly, he supported a policy that increased efforts to smuggle into the U.S.S.R. written material regarding freedom and democracy, as well as the works of the dissidents themselves, such as Alexander Solzhenitsyn's *The Gulag Archipelago*. Carter also covertly aided programs designed to maintain the heritage of ethnic minorities of America's cold war adversary by infiltrating information regarding Russian history and culture.

Carter also imposed certain economic sanctions on the Soviets after they placed famous dissidents Anatoliy Shcharansky and Aleksandr Ginzberg on trial. Following the Soviet invasion of Afghanistan, more severe economic sanctions were placed on the U.S.S.R. by Carter, which set the table for Ronald Reagan to inflict even more economic measures on the Soviets.

Gates wrote that there existed a greater level of disdain between the U.S. and U.S.S.R. than was the case under all the chief executives of the Cold War except for Harry Truman, and that does not exclude Reagan. While many Americans and Europeans didn't see it, the Soviets believed Carter had discarded the rules that had formed the relationship during the Cold War, and had proceeded boldly on a mission of confrontation and challenge.

Gates asserted that, in his view, the Soviets considered Carter to be a dangerous ideological opponent and also a geopolitical threat—and as a president ready to act on his hostility in those areas. That perception came in stark contrast to the demonstrated policies of previous American presidents dating back to Eisenhower. Gates wrote, "...the Soviets immediately recognized this for the fundamental challenge it was: they believed he sought to overthrow their system...the Soviet leaders knew the implications for them of what Carter was doing, and hated him for it." The former CIA director also sensed the Soviets eventually recognized a definite continuity between Carter's rhetoric and policies pertaining to them and the rhetoric and policies of Reagan. Furthermore, Gates claimed, Carter set the table for Reagan in the strategic arena, in "...confronting the Soviets and Cubans in the Third World, and in challenging the legitimacy of Soviet authority at home. He took the first steps to strip away the mask of Soviet ascendancy and exploit the reality of Soviet vulnerability…"

STRATEGIC FORCES

Carter assumed the presidency after a period when U.S. defense spending declined in real terms every year from 1968 through 1976. Under Carter's leadership, this decline was reversed, and his lead encouraged increases by America's allies. During Carter's term, the U.S. either maintained or started modernization programs, with the exception of the B-1 bomber—that became the foundation of American strategic strength from Reagan on forward. Crucial programs for NATO modernization began on Carter's watch and the first commitment was made to deploy in tandem nuclear cruise missiles along with the Pershing II IRBMs in Europe.

Carter ordered the strengthening of all major components of U.S. strategic forces. The cruise missile modernized American strategic air deterrent. B-52 capabilities were upgraded, enhancing its ability to attack heavily defended targets.

Carter also updated the U.S. strategic submarine force. Four POSEIDON submarines equipped with new, 4,000 mile TRIDENT I missiles were deployed in 1980, as were nine TRIDENT submarines.

The M-X missile program, supported by Carter, improved U.S. land-based intercontinental ballistic missile capabilities. Technical advancements in the basing design brought added operational benefits, reduced costs, and a softened environmental impact.

STRATEGIC DOCTRINE

Carter set his strategic doctrine in motion soon after taking office, when he commissioned a comprehensive net evaluation. He presented his strategic doctrine in a variety of connected and mutually supporting Presidential Directives. Their broad theme was to provide a doctrinal basis, and the definitive program to implement it, that informed the world that no potential enemy of the United States would ever deduce that the results of his aggression would be worth our enormous retaliatory response.

These policies were devised, principally, to deter Soviet aggression; not just Soviet the military itself but specifically Soviet military doctrine. Carter's strategic doctrine was undertaken with proper consultation with America's NATO Allies, and remained totally consistent with NATO's strategy of flexible response.

FORCES FOR NATO

Carter directed an acceleration in U.S. ability to supply Western Europe with massive ground and air forces in times of emergency. He commissioned a major modernization upgrade for the Army's weapons and equipment, providing more armor, firepower, and tactical mobility.

He ordered the placing of more heavy equipment in Europe to be battle-ready for attacks with little warning, and greatly enhanced U.S. airlift and sealift capabilities.

Carter also increased American tactical air forces, purchasing about 1700 new fighter and attack aircraft, while raising the amount of Air Force fighter wings by over 10 percent.

SECURITY ASSISTANCE

While strengthening U.S. defense capabilities, Carter also commanded that America would remain vigilant in assisting other countries in retaining their own security and independence. He noted that events since World War II, up to that time centered on Southwest Asia, clearly illustrated that U.S. security cannot be risked in a go-it-alone philosophy, and that our country's opportunities for peace are closely linked to those of our allies.

Carter's programs enhanced U.S. security in two primary ways. First, they helped our allies to develop the means to defend themselves and retain their own independence. An example during Carter's term was the rapid support given Thailand to help secure that nation's defenses against the thousands of Soviet-backed Vietnamese troops that were positioned on its eastern frontier. Also, Carter's policies were welcomed by allies such as Israel, Greece, Turkey and South Korea. Second, Carter's security assistance comprised an essential element in the broad mutually beneficial relationships that the U.S. had long established with many countries which allowed either U.S. bases on their land or access by the U.S. military to their facilities (the importance of which was illustrated in the two ensuing Gulf Wars). These programs were especially important with regard to the 1980 access agreements with several nations in the Persian Gulf and Indian Ocean regions and have been vital to the protection of U.S. interests throughout Southwest Asia.

RAPID DEPLOYMENT FORCES

Carter set in motion the policy that enhanced U.S. ability to react rapidly to non-NATO emergencies wherever needed by our commitments or when American interests are endangered.

The rapid deployment forces organized under Carter were flexible to an unprecedented degree: They varied in size from several ships or air squadrons to formations as high as 100,000 soldiers.

Among the specific initiatives Carter implemented to facilitate a U.S. response to crises beyond Europe were:

* the construction of a new fleet of huge cargo aircraft with intercontinental range;
* the organization and procurement of a contingent of Maritime Prepositioning Ships that will transport heavy equipment and provisions for three Marine Corps brigades;
* the commissioning of fast sealift ships to move large amounts of soldiers and material quickly from the U.S. to overseas regions of deployment;

In addition, America's European allies during Carter's term agreed on the necessity of lending support to U.S. deployments in Southwest Asia.

NAVAL FORCES

The shipbuilding program Carter envisioned assured the ability of the U.S. Navy to operate in high-risk areas, to keep control of the seas and guard vital lines of communication and to provide the robust maritime abilities of U.S. deployment forces. Carter deemed this mandatory for operations in far-removed regions of the earth, where it could not be always predicted well in advance the precise area of trouble, or preposition supplies on land.

MILITARY PERSONNEL

Carter called for the largest peacetime raise ever seen in military pay and allowances. He boosted U.S. preparedness and combat endurance by improving the Reserve Components. All reservists were targeted to units designed to complement and offer the required depth to American active forces.

THE U.S. AND THE PACIFIC NATIONS

Normalization of U.S. relations with China led to China's joining the international community and began a productive Chinese role in the Asia-Pacific region. Carter established a process of frequent and frank consultations between the U.S. and Chinese governments, demonstrated by several high-level visits and by constant exchanges at the working level, through which both countries were able to identify increasingly wide areas of common interest on which better relations could be built.

American relations with the Association of Southeast Asian Nations (ASEAN) also expanded considerably during Carter's term. ASEAN became the focus for U.S. policy in Southeast Asia, and its cohesion and strength were seen as essential to stability in this vital area and beyond.

Carter strengthened our alliance with South Korea and helped guarantee its security during a difficult time of political transition.

Carter amended America's military base agreement with the Philippines, assuring stable access to these bases through 1991. This action tied in American Philippine bases to the strategic flexibility of U.S. forces and U.S. access to the Indian Ocean.

MIDDLE EAST

In the Middle East, Carter's determination to consolidate what was achieved in the peace process—and to enhance that accomplishment with continued progress toward a comprehensive peace settlement—remained a central goal of his foreign policy. During Carter's administration Egypt and Israel made steady progress in the normalization of their relations in numerous fields, giving the benefits of peace directly to their citizens. The relationship established between Egypt and Israel during Carter's term, and the resulting Camp David Accords, stand as an example of peaceful cooperation in a constantly fragmented and turbulent region.

PERSIAN GULF

Long before the Gulf Wars, Carter instituted the Carter Doctrine to protect America's vital interests in the Persian Gulf and to reinforce the trust and confidence of America's allies in the region in our ability to come to their aid rapidly with American military force if needed. Carter increased America's naval presence in the Indian Ocean. He also ordered the creation of a Rapid Deployment Force which could move immediately to the Gulf—

or any other region of the world where outside aggression threatened. Carter entered into agreements with countries that enabled the U.S. to use their airports and naval facilities in an emergency, the importance of which was illustrated in both Gulf Wars. Carter approved reasonable amounts of American weaponry for regional countries which wanted the ability to defend themselves.

SOUTH ASIA

The Soviet invasion of Afghanistan presented a new challenge to this region, and especially to neighboring Pakistan. Carter engaged in a constant dialogue with the Pakistan government regarding its development and security requirements and the economic burden stemming from Afghan refugees who fled to Pakistan. The Carter Administration remained committed to Pakistan's territorial integrity and independence.

Activities in the broad South/Southwest Asian region also revealed a new importance to America's relations with India, the largest and strongest power in the region. Indian policies and perceptions, though often at odds with America's, didn't stop Carter from engaging in a candid dialogue with this sister democracy, in order to prevent misunderstandings that sometimes complicated relations between the two countries.

Carter attached much importance to strong economic assistance programs to the nations in the region, which included a majority of the poor of the non-Communist countries. Carter stated that these programs would help achieve stability in the area, an objective shared with the affected countries. Great progress was achieved by these nations in increasing food production; international efforts to harness the great river resources of South Asia was a Carter initiative that helped increase energy production.

AFRICA

Under Carter, America achieved a new level of trust and cooperation with Africa. His efforts, along with U.S. allies, to bring peace in southern Africa, America's increased efforts to assist the poorest nations in Africa in fighting poverty, and expanded efforts by the U.S. to promote trade and investment encouraged growing respect for America and to cooperation in areas of major interest to the United States.

Since Africa contains many of the mineral resources vital for the American economy, Carter stressed the necessity of helping the African countries solve their problems of poverty and of forging stronger ties between the American private sector and African economies. American assistance to Africa increased by more than double during Carter's four years in office. Equally important, he ordered new mechanisms for private investment and trade.

Nigeria, the second largest oil supplier to America, was of particular importance to Carter. During his Administration there was a greatly expanded and improved relationship with Nigeria and other West African nations whose aspirations for a constitutional democratic order were fully supported by America. This interest was illustrated by the visit of Vice President Mondale to West Africa in July of 1980 and the visit to Washington of the President of Nigeria in October, 1980. During Vice President Mondale's trip, a Joint Agricultural Consultative Committee was created, with the U.S. represented totally by the private sector.

Another tenet of the Carter Administration's approach to African problems was the support for regional solutions to Africa's problems. Carter supported initiatives by the Organization of African Unity to solve the continued conflict in the western Sahara, Chad, and the Horn. In southern Africa Carter pursued a policy of calling for peaceful development toward majority rule.

In 1980, Southern Rhodesia became independent as Zimbabwe, a multiracial country under a constitution of majority rule. Zimbabwean independence marked the culmination of a long struggle within the nation and diplomatic efforts involving America, Great Britain, and African states neighboring Zimbabwe.

In appreciation for Carter's active concern with issues of importance to Africans, African states cooperated with the U.S. on issues of importance to America's national interests. African states voted overwhelmingly in favor of the U.N. Resolution demanding the release of the U.S. hostages in Iran, and for the U.N. Resolution condemning the Soviet invasion of Afghanistan. Two countries of Africa signed access agreements with Carter allowing our use of naval and air facilities in the Indian Ocean.

Due to Carter's efforts, Africans became increasingly vocal on human rights. African leaders spoke out on the topic of political prisoners, and the OAU drafted its own Charter on Human Rights. During Carter's last year in office, three countries in Africa—Nigeria, Ghana, and Uganda—returned to civilian rule.

Liberia, a nation of long-standing ties with America and the site of considerable U.S. investment and facilities, saw a coup take place in 1980, leading to a period of political and economic uncertainty. Carter acted swiftly to meet this situation, urging the release of political prisoners, and many were set free; Carter directed that emergency economic assistance be rendered to help avoid economic collapse. He called for the IMF and the banking community to instill economic stability; his administration worked closely with Liberia's new leaders to maintain that country's strong ties with the West and to guard America's vital interests.

NORTH AFRICA

In 1979, after a Libyan-inspired commando assault on a Tunisian provincial city, Carter responded promptly to Tunisia's urgent request for aid, both by ordering the airlifting of needed military equipment and by reiterating our longstanding interest in the security and integrity of this friend of the U.S. Carter consistently opposed other irresponsible Libyan actions. Seeing no opportunity to engage in a productive dialogue with the Libyan government, Carter closed down the embassy in Libya and later approved the expelling of six Libyan diplomats in Washington for the purpose of stopping an intimidation campaign against Libyan citizens in the U.S.

Under Carter, U.S. relations with Algeria improved, and that nation played a crucial role as intermediary between Iran and the U.S. during the hostage crisis.

LATIN AMERICA AND THE CARIBBEAN

The principles of Carter's policies in this region were consistent throughout his term. First, he supported democracy and promoted human rights. Second, he launched a successful campaign help rid the hemisphere of both repression and terrorism. Third, he respected ideological diversity and did not condone outside intervention in strictly internal affairs. Fourth, he announced a U.S. commitment to act in response to a request for help by a country under threat of attack. And fifth, he backed social and economic development within a democratic framework.

During Carter's term, his administration's quiet diplomacy bore significant fruit, with an undeniable trend in favor of democracy in this region. Peru began a democratically elected government. In Central America, Hondurans cast ballots in record numbers in their first national elections in over eight years. In the Caribbean seven elections returned governments strongly committed to the democratic trend of the Commonwealth.

The Caribbean Group for Cooperation in Economic Development, which Carter established with 29 other countries in 1977, directed $750 million in external financing for growth in the Caribbean. Carter fully supported the formation of Caribbean/ Central American Action, a private sector organization that became a major force in improving people-to-people bonds, and enhancing the role of private enterprise in the development of democratic societies.

Under Carter, a new partnership was created with Panama; that country became a model for nations of all sizes. The longstanding issue of American control over the canal in Panamanian territory, that was the source of severe resentment on the part of Panama, was resolved. The security of the canal was bolstered, while canal employees, American and Panamanian alike, remained on the job and saw their living and working conditions virtually unaffected.

In 1980, relations with Mexico continued to improve due in large measure to the effectiveness of Carter's support for the Coordinator for Mexican Affairs and the increased use of the U.S.-Mexico Consultative Mechanism. By conducting periodic meetings of its numerous working groups, Carter was able to prevent mutual concerns from becoming serious issues. The office of the Coordinator implemented Carter's order to all agencies to accord top priority to Mexican concerns. Trade with Mexico increased by almost 60 percent to nearly $30 billion, making that nation America's third largest trading partner.

HUMAN RIGHTS

The human rights policy of the United States was an integral part of Carter's overall foreign policy. This policy served the national interest of America in several important ways: by encouraging respect by nations for the basic rights of human beings, it promoted peaceful, constructive change, lowered the likelihood of internal pressures for violent change and for the exploitation of these by America's adversaries, and therefore directly served America's long-term interest in peace and stability; by matching the trumpeting of fundamental American principles of freedom with specific foreign policy actions, Carter's Administration shined in vivid contrast to America's ideological opponents; by Carter's efforts to expand freedom elsewhere, he made our own freedom, and our own nation, more secure. Carter clearly demonstrated that nations that respect human rights make stronger allies and closer friends.

Carter's human rights achievements were considerable during his administration:

* Free elections were conducted and democratic governments installed in Peru, Dominica, and Jamaica. Honduras had a free election for installation of a constituent assembly.

* The "Charter of Conduct" championed by Carter and signed in Riobamba, Ecuador, by Ecuador, Colombia, Venezuela, Peru, Costa Rica, Panama and Spain, confirmed the importance of democracy and human rights for the Andean countries.

* The Organization of American States, in its yearly General Assembly, passed a resolution in support of the Inter-American Human Rights Commission's work.

Carter, of course, would not accept credit for these numerous developments. But over 20 years of hindsight reveals that Carter's policies encouraged and likely influenced these events.

Carter insisted that those who saw a contradiction between U.S. security and America's humanitarian interests forgot that the basis for a secure and stable society is the bond of trust between a government and its citizens. He profoundly believed that the world's future would not be found in authoritarianism; instead, his goal was to steer the globe towards the human face of democracy, the human voice of individual liberty, and the human hand of economic development.

Former CIA Director Robert Gates noted that "…even though Carter's human rights policies were derided at home as naïve and counterproductive, in later years Soviet dissidents would be virtually unanimous in their praise of those policies and the importance to the democratic dissidents of the publicity those policies brought their cause…his approach marked a decisive and historic turning point in the U.S.-Soviet relationship."

NON-PROLIFERATION

Carter's Administration was committed to stemming the spread of nuclear weapons. He succeeded on three fronts:

* First, Carter encouraged other nations to accede to the non-Proliferation Treaty. Carter also actively called upon other nations to accept full-scope safeguards on all of their nuclear activities and asked other nuclear suppliers to accept a full-scope safeguards requirement as a condition for future supply.
* Second, the International Nuclear Fuel Cycle Evaluation (INFCE), which Carter supported and was completed in 1980, demonstrated that suppliers and recipients could work together on these technically complex and sensitive issues.
* And third, Carter encouraged regional cooperation and restraint. This led to a treaty which contributed to the lowering of nuclear dangers for Latin American nations.

SEVEN

(UN)CONVENTIONAL WISDOM AND UNANSWERED QUESTIONS

First and foremost, I no longer feel there is a necessity to view the Carter presidency and post-presidency as two mutually exclusive entities. When taken in its totality, Carter's record is overwhelming in its scope of achievement.

The reader will notice I did not survey voters about a potential Bush-Carter election. I figured there was no use of getting ahead of the first order of business, and that is demonstrating to Democrats and to independent swing voters that he can win the nomination convincingly.

Carter is almost without a doubt the only person in America who would have to decide if he can accomplish more as president or as a private citizen. The Carter Center's unique niche in world affairs may ultimately sway him to decline the opportunity to run for the Democratic nomination.

The vast majority of senior citizens, especially those who have a comfortable retirement plan, eventually decide to rest on their laurels and enjoy their golden years free of working concerns. Carter would have to decide if he is willing to go in the exact opposite direction and serve his country for another four years, into his mid-80s. His role model here could be his mother, Miss Lillian, who went to India as a member of the Peace Corps when she was in her late 60s.

Democrats may be wise to frame their foreign policy platform by acknowledging while Bush may have been an effective president in winning the war in Iraq, Carter is the best man to win the peace in the Middle East, by virtue of his immense standing in the region.

An attack on Carter's economic record as president would be largely negated unless the economy of mid-2003 improves markedly by late 2004. A domestic-record argument that resorts to Republicans saying in effect, "Carter's economy was worse than Bush's economy" would make little impact.

Carter could prove to be the most relaxed candidate ever to be nominated by a major party for president, by virtue of his advanced years, his prestige, and the sheer fact that he would enter the race having nothing to lose.

Bush would have a definite dilemma in facing Carter: how to avoid appearing overly aggressive in countering Carter's views while simultaneously not appearing to be too deferential.

A Carter-Bush debate would be an unprecedented event: it would almost seem surreal having both participants addressed by the media panel as "Mr. President."

The Democrats could stress that Carter is likely the only man alive to be praised by the Egyptians, Israelis and Palistineans (in the aftermath of winning the 2002 Nobel Peace Prize).

Carter would have to be prepared to rebut an assertion by Bush that he (Bush) simply invoked the Carter Doctrine with the attack on Iraq. The Carter Doctrine stated that the U.S. would be prepared to use military force in the event of a threat to our interests in the Persian Gulf region; the implication by Bush would be that Carter would not have adhered to his own doctrine, preferring to pursue the peace negotiations he's been renowned for over the last 25 years.

Carter can show fairness by defending Bush on his State of the Union error, when he was given inaccurate information regarding Iraq's actions in seeking weapons of mass destruction, yet at the same time remind the public that his anti-war assertion—that the Bush Administration did not prove the existence of these weapons in Iraq on the eve of the war—has proven correct.

Carter would most certainly be questioned about his opinion of Bush's actions regarding the war on terrorism, how his reaction to September 11 would have differed from Bush's, and how he would proceed in the war on terror that Bush has made by necessity the defining issue of his Administration.

The perception of Carter being indecisive during his term is dismissed by his former budget director, Bert Lance, in his book, *The Truth of the Matter*, as being patently false. He wrote:

"There wasn't any incompetence or vacillation involved in (Carter's) having the imagination and decisiveness to create the federal executive service, the new system to attract more top-flight executives to government service by providing more opportunities for advancement. Or in deregulating the airlines to create stiffer competition and thus lower airfares for the people of the United States. Or in holding the budget to one-tenth of what Reagan allowed to happen…"

Carter, noted Lance, as far back as his days as the governor of Georgia, was called anything but a vacillator:

"He was criticized for being just the opposite—too strong willed, bullheaded, even too decisive. Folks said (and they were right) that once he made up his mind to do something after hearing all sides, he went ahead and did it and stuck to his decision. That's not my definition of a vacillator, and I don't think it's anybody else's either." Lance's observations about Carter echo the contemporary complaints about President Truman.

Carter can't be perceived as an economic liberal; his battles with the Democratic Congress during his term is evidence of that. As recently as July, 2003, at Bob Dole's 80th birthday celebration, Carter stated that he thought he had more in common with the Republicans on economic issues while he was in office than with his own party.

Carter passed a higher percentage of legislation than JFK or LBJ.

For those who put stock in such matters, Carter by many accounts has the highest standing abroad of any living American.

For those who liked the economic policies of the Clinton Administration while not necessarily respecting Bill Clinton himself, Carter could attract the support of those voters—assuming he pursues much of Clinton's economic agenda—and by his stature, Carter would also claim their respect.

If Carter did seek and win a second term, it would be highly interesting to see if and how he would utilize the heretofore non-partisan Carter Center, considering its record of diplomatic success and humanitarian achievements dating back to the mid-1980s. Would he have the State Department integrate the Carter Center's "Track 1.5" diplomacy, into some areas of official foreign policy? ("Track 1.5" diplomacy, as it is referred to at the Carter Center, is essentially, informal, behind-the-scenes discussions and negotiations, but is accompanied by unique access due to Carter's status, more than is available in "Track-two" diplomacy).

Or would the emphasis of the Carter Center, in the event of Carter's re-election, be placed in advancing the Center's humanitarian works? Can a non-partisan organization function when its founder is an active partisan (as is any president) in the broad sense of the word?

Would Carter's post-presidency allow the media to now view him in a more positive light than he was portrayed during his Administration?

If Carter pursued and received the Democratic nomination, who would be his best choice as a running mate? Would he strongly consider retired General Wesley Clark, should Clark's own presidential bid come up short? (Clark entered the race shortly before *Welcome Back, Carter* went to press).

What would be Carter's electoral strategy? Could he win a state or two in the Republican solid South while keeping the bulk of states that voted for Al Gore in 2000?

Would Carter have the ability to keep pace with President Bush in the crucial area of fundraising? Even if he can't match Bush dollar for dollar, I suspect there won't be a wide enough discrepancy to make a difference on Election Day.

Would Carter, for reasons stated earlier, actually decline running for the nomination, if ensuing polls show him with a commanding lead among Democrats?

Would one of Carter's first acts if elected be to end the trade embargo against Cuba and restore full diplomatic relations with the Castro regime? That would be reminiscent of a bold stroke he undertook in his first act as president in 1977, when he pardoned all Vietnam draft dodgers.

Would a revised energy policy be one of Carter's core campaign issues?

What role would Al Gore play in a Carter campaign and Administration?

Would Carter pursue a universal health care bill that would be more acceptable to Congress than Hillary Clinton's plan? Or does the existence of a Republican Congress make that issue a non-starter?

Would the age issue merit much public and media concern, or is Carter so obviously vigorous that his age would actually be considered by many to be a plus, because of his acquired wisdom?

Would Carter have enough voting strength among women and minorities to offset Bush's vastly superior numbers among white men?

With the current natural gas crisis, it appears as if Carter was prophetic in his insistence on passing an energy bill when he was president, even though the bill didn't go as far as he would have liked. Although he'd never do it, Carter seemingly has every right to say "I told you so" in regards to future energy shortages.

A new Internet Web Site has emerged during the writing of this book called carterforpresident.org. Will the media note the efforts of this grass-roots organization?

Will Carter offer any encouragement—or discouragement—to efforts made on his behalf to raise his name as the best candidate for the Democratic nomination, and wait and see if nationally recognized pollsters uncover results similar to those seen in *Welcome Back, Carter?*

EIGHT

THE EMBODIMENT OF MOST PRESIDENTS

In Mr. *President: The Human Side of America's Chief Executives*, author David Rubel relates characteristics of all U.S. presidents that are evidenced in the multi-faceted Jimmy Carter. In a sense, Carter is a living compilation of our most of our nation's presidents, as seen by the following comparisons.

George Washington thought of himself primarily as a farmer; he felt that his work in bettering farming techniques was as vital as he ever did for the United States. Carter, who feels at one with the land of his forefathers, is equally proud of his farming heritage.

Plenty of his associates were put off by John Adam's self-righteousness. But when a crisis arose, as occurred almost daily during the fight for independence by the colonies, that trait proved to be a valuable asset to Adams; a weaker-willed man could have very well decided that life under

King George's rule was just fine, and would not have supported the revolution. Carter's critics have made the same claim about him, but again, this mainly is a comment about Carter possessing the courage of his convictions, which is what the Republicans always loved about Reagan.

The supporters of Thomas Jefferson were amazed by his agile mind. They often spoke of how they were taken aback by the scope of his knowledge and the nobility of his aspirations. Over his lifetime, Jefferson retained an eager curiosity for almost every category of human knowledge. These comments can easily have been made about Carter.

Vital to James Madison's success was his firm understanding of complicated issues. It was often said that Carter knew more about the bills that were proposed in Congress than the bill's author, much to the chagrin of many members of Congress.

James Monroe's qualities of innate goodness and his authentic concern for the feelings of others was best described by Jefferson to Madison in 1787: "Turn his soul wrong side inwards and there is not a spot on it." Do many doubt the same is essentially true about Carter?

An uncompromising work ethic kept John Quincy Adams on the go from 5 a.m. until almost midnight. He decided matters not because the public favored a certain course of action, but because he believed his decisions were correct. His post-presidency brought him (and later, William Howard Taft) more respect and acclaim than he received during his term in the White House. The same can be said of Carter in regards to all these observations about JQA.

Andrew Jackson saw himself as a man of the people, as was demonstrated by inviting the public to the White House after his inauguration. Carter regarded himself the same way, most vividly in his walk down Pennsylvania Avenue with his family after he took the oath of office.

William Henry Harrison was considered a leading humanitarian of his era, even if the word "humanitarian" was not yet in vogue. As Indiana's governor from 1800 to 1812, he was recognized for his even-handed and compassionate concern for the welfare of Indians.

James K. Polk referred to himself in his diary as the "hardest working man in America." He knew first hand almost all details of his Administration. Carter, who is said to have worked like an indentured servant in the White House, also preferred a "hands-on" approach to events in his Administration.

Zachary Taylor was seen as direct and stubborn, unpretentious and kind, and was an honest man who scorned political machinations. This is Carter all over again.

James Buchanan comported himself with the highest degree of dignity, and meticulously steered clear of any conflict of interest between his politics and finances. Carter never demeaned his office, and was never accused of personal gain during his career of public service.

Abraham Lincoln announced the emancipation the slaves in the Old South; just over a century later, as Georgia governor, Carter called for an official end to all forms of segregation in the New South.

From the days of his youth, Andrew Johnson was appalled by discrepancy between the affluent over common citizens. Carter has been called the ever-widening gap between rich and poor nations one of the major threats to world peace.

Rutherford Hayes and his wife Lucy didn't live a rich lifestyle. Their mission in life was a devotion to public service. Hayes, a devout Christian, called on White House guests to sing hymns in the White House. The Carters have maintained as their residence a modest brick ranch in Plains, Georgia; and Carter taught a Sunday school class while he was president.

James Garfield was a religious and scholarly individual, who defined greatness in a man with a question: "Did he drift unresistingly on the currents of life, or did he lead the thoughts of men to higher and nobler purposes?" Carter's high-minded activism fits under Garfield's definition of greatness.

Chester Arthur was called an "extremely tender-hearted man" upon his death, and presided over an honest and efficient government. Here is Carter once again.

Author David Rubel's summary of Grover Cleveland appears to describe Carter precisely: "Cleveland performed admirably, but his introverted manner hurt him politically. He was hard-working, conscientious and methodical, yet could also be stubborn. He brought a high standard of personal integrity to government service."

Benjamin Harrison disdained the deal-making and buttonholing that occurred daily in Congress. Carter was much the same, preferring to take his case on various issues directly to the people.

William McKinley adhered to a "divine loving-kindness," and this faith provided him with an inner serenity that he carried his whole life. These traits are also obvious in the born-again Carter.

In addition to winning the Nobel Peace Prize, Theodore Roosevelt had over 75 million acres of forest placed under federal protection. Carter's Alaska Lands Act set aside 97 million acres of parks and refuges, the largest protective land act in U.S. history.

Woodrow Wilson, the other president besides TR and Carter to win the Nobel Peace Prize, strongly adhered to his Christian beliefs. He mostly portrayed a serious demeanor, and set high standards for the United States. Carter has been often described as a latter-day Wilson, for obvious reasons.

Herbert Hoover, like Carter, was an engineer—in Hoover's case, a mining engineer—and was also regarded one of the great humanitarians of the 20th century. Working without any government aid, he organized the Committee for the Relief of Belgium, raising a billion dollars to feed and clothe that impoverished nation after World War I, and led a similar effort to feed several European countries after World War II. Carter, as was chronicled earlier, has had substantial success in taking on agricultural and health issues in many African nations. Hoover's love of fishing was equaled by Carter's; both wrote entertaining books on the sport of angling. Fishing, to Hoover, was "a pursuit of almost spiritual intensity," according to his biographer Richard Norton Smith, a sentiment that fully describes Carter's passion for the sport.

Franklin D. Roosevelt's personality was virtually a stark opposite to Carter's, but the New Deal programs of the 1930's have always been regarded by Carter as an inspired and necessary response to the economic collapse this nation endured during the Great Depression. Carter received the Four Freedoms Award on the 50th anniversary of FDR's death, on April 12, 1995, in a ceremony at the Little White House in Warm Springs, Georgia. In his acceptance speech, Douglas Brinkley wrote in *The Unfinished Presidency*, Carter spoke from the heart when he related how difficult times were for small farmers in rural Georgia, and "…he celebrated the bold civil and human rights achievements of Eleanor Roosevelt, and what he saw as FDR's most lasting achievement—the United Nations."

Harry Truman, Carter believed, was "The greatest president of the 20th century." In an oral history arranged by the Harry S Truman National Historic Site, Carter also said, "He was honest. He told the truth, even when it was painful. He didn't try to duck an important issue because it might cost him a few points in the public opinion polls." These are all descriptions that fit Carter. Truman's standing in those polls sunk to record lows because of the combination of high inflation and America's continuing stand-off in the Korean War. Carter, of course, was victimized by high inflation that peaked in his last year in office, and by the Iranian hostage crisis. Truman's popularity soared in the next generation, as Carter's has a generation after leaving office.

Dwight Eisenhower was the only American president of the 20th century who had a lengthier military career than Carter's service in the U.S. Navy from 1943-54. Ike's middle of the road philosophy to domestic spending also coincided with Carter's views. Ike also was an avid fisherman along the lines of Hoover and Carter.

The Peace Corps, widely seen as the greatest legacy of John F. Kennedy, was an inspiration and model for the Carter Center Health Programs. Miss Lillian, President Carter's mother, joined the Peace Corps at age 68, felt the most important work of her life took place as a Peace Corps volunteer in India.

Lyndon Johnson had "the rare gift to mobilize the powers of government to raise up the downtrodden," said his biographer Robert Caro. Carter has similarly learned to do the same through the powers of the corporate world.

Richard Nixon's opening to China gave Carter the opportunity to normalize relations with China in 1979, and Carter praised Nixon for this great achievement.

Gerald Ford's inherent decency and integrity were the hallmarks of his Administration. Carter, having the same virtues, has been honored to team with Ford in issuing joint statements on several critical issues of the past two decades.

As noted earlier, Ronald Reagan continued Carter's build up of the U.S. military in response to Soviet aggression. Both attacked the legitimacy of Communist rule, leading to the end of the Cold War.

George H. W. Bush and Carter both highly support the idea of personal diplomacy—striking up friendships or at least a rapport—with leaders around the world as a means to facilitate global objectives and prevent misunderstandings that are otherwise avoidable.

In Douglas Brinkley's *The Unfinished Presidency*, Bill Clinton—another polar opposite from Carter in terms of style—is quoted as saying, "If you look at President Carter's achievement by establishing the Carter Center and having not just a library, but an active, vibrant place where he could promote agricultural development and fight disease and advance democracy and human rights and monitor elections and all the things he's done, I mean, there's really almost no parallel for it in the history of the country. He is a great resource that ought to be used to the benefit of the country wherever possible."

The case presented in *Welcome Back, Carter* suggests that Democrats should strongly consider whether that place is in the White House

EPILOGUE

Welcome Back, Carter went to press on the eve of the 25th anniversary of President Carter's mediation of the Camp David Accords between Egypt and Israel. This is rightfully acclaimed as President Carter's greatest achievement, yet the volatility in the Middle East in the early 21st century shows just how far away that region of the world remains from any semblance of a lasting peace. The liberation of the Iraqi people from Saddam Hussein has removed one of the most brutal dictators in recent memory, but the U.S. occupation of Iraq has also heightened resentment of America amongst a vast majority of Middle Eastern nations.

President Bush's war on terror remains his number one priority, and his call for the destruction of the al-Queda organization and its allies in the wake of the heinous attacks of September 11 has been widely supported by the American people. While great progress has been made on that front, the U.S. road map to peace in the Middle East is in danger of being cast aside in its entirety, as evidenced by the continued suicide attacks on Israel by Hamas, the Palistinean terror group.

As noted earlier, Jimmy Carter has far and away the highest standing of any American in the Middle East, and history has proven that his credibility would offer the best chance of an agreement between these two bitter adversaries. How Carter would conduct a war on terror is subject for considerable speculation, but of course he would certainly need to address that national priority during any attempt for the Democratic nomination and the presidency.

For those who approve the war on terrorist organizations, but disapprove of the exaggerated justifications for invading Iraq; for those who feel that while the liberation of Iraq from Saddam Hussein was a worthy cause, but unwittingly further inflamed the tinderbox that is the Middle East; for those who seriously question whether President Bush can ever obtain the respect and prestige necessary to preside over a Middle East peace agreement; and for those who have lost faith in the Bush economic plan, with the elimination of nearly three million jobs in the U.S. since he assumed office:

No Democrat could frame a more vivid alternative to the policies of the Bush Administration than former President Jimmy Carter. Not only is he regarded by acclamation as the world's preeminent champion of human rights; but his stature in the eyes of the world—the highest of any American—is bolstered by an unassailable integrity, and his works on behalf of the impoverished, the disease-ridden, and those who simply desire to live in peace and a democratic society have provided a greater clarity of the goals of his first term in office. His disciplined and active lifestyle has enabled him to age gracefully, and he has admitted on many occasions how much better a president he would have been if he knew then all that he knows now as a result of a long and productive life. *Shouldn't wisdom be considered the most essential presidential attribute? And if that's the case, there's no doubt that Carter should be the Democratic nominee.*

Regarding domestic policy, any Democratic president who cancelled pork-barrel Democratic water projects can never be considered a tax-and-spend liberal; to the contrary, stories of Carter's tightness with a dollar are legendary among his friends. As previously mentioned, Carter's tell-it-like-it-is-manner evokes memories of Harry Truman, his favorite predecessor;

while Truman's predecessor, Franklin D. Roosevelt, once provided a statement that has come to best summarize the world view held by Jimmy Carter: "Governments can err, presidents do make mistakes, but the immortal Dante tells us that divine Justice weighs the sins of the cold-blooded and the sins of the warm hearted in different scales. Better the occasional faults of a government that lives in a spirit of charity than the constant omissions of a government frozen in the ice of its own indifference."

So, having been stunned by my own survey results, and then being taken aback by Carter's lengthy record of achievement, I admit to deviating from my traditional independent leanings to becoming an unabashed Carter partisan. I think the remaining question should not be why Democrats would want Jimmy Carter as their 2004 presidential nominee—but rather, why not? He's already made a world of difference.

Welcome Back, Carter
2004 Democratic Presidential Poll Winner

POSTSCRIPT

Just before going to press, I learned that Jimmy Carter was asked offstage at a public event if he would ever consider another run for the White House. He gave his standard answer that no, he had no ambition to be president again, and besides, the Democrats already had an outstanding collection of candidates. He was then asked if no one emerged as the front-runner in the early Democratic primaries, would he respond to a "Draft Carter" movement if one ever materialized, if his support was verified in the polls. It was confirmed to me by an authoritative source that the former president smiled and replied, "Well, that would be another story."